THE GREEK TRAGEDY
IN NEW TRANSLATIONS

GENERAL EDITORS
William Arrowsmith and Herbert Golder

EURIPIDES: Suppliant Women

EURIPIDES

Suppliant Women

Translated by
ROSANNA WARREN
and
STEPHEN SCULLY

New York Oxford
OXFORD UNIVERSITY PRESS
1995

Oxford University Press

Oxford   New York
Athens   Auckland   Bangkok   Bombay
Calcutta   Cape Town   Dar es Salaam   Delhi
Florence   Hong Kong   Istanbul   Karachi
Kuala Lumpur   Madras   Madrid   Melbourne
Mexico City   Nairobi   Paris   Singapore
Taipei   Tokyo   Toronto

and associated companies in
Berlin   Ibadan

Copyright © 1995 by Rosanna Warren and Stephen Scully

Published by Oxford University Press, Inc.
200 Madison Avenue, New York, New York 10016

Oxford is a registered trademark of Oxford University Press

Library of Congress Cataloging-in-Publication Data
Euripides.
[Supplices. English]
Suppliant women / Euripides ; translated by Rosanna Warren and Stephen Scully.
p. cm.—(Greek tragedy in new translations)
ISBN 0-19-504553-X (pbk.)
1. Seven against Thebes (Greek mythology)—Drama.
2. Adrastus (Greek mythology)—Drama.
3. Theseus (Greek mythology)—Drama.
I. Warren, Rosanna.   II. Scully, Stephen, 1947–
III. Title.   IV. Series.
PA3975.S9W37 1995
883'.01—dc20   94-14161

9 8 7 6 5 4 3 2 1

Printed in the United States of America
on acid-free paper

For Benjamin, Katherine, Chiara

EDITORS' FOREWORD

The Greek Tragedy in New Translations is based on the conviction that poets like Aeschylus, Sophocles, and Euripides can only be properly rendered by translators who are themselves poets. Scholars may, it is true, produce useful and perceptive versions. But our most urgent present need is for a *re-creation* of these plays—as though they had been written, freshly and greatly, by masters fully at home in the English of our own times. Unless the translator is a poet, his original is likely to reach us in crippled form: deprived of the power and pertinence it must have if it is to speak to us of what is permanent in the Greek. But poetry is not enough; the translator must obviously *know* what he is doing, or he is bound to do it badly. Clearly, few contemporary poets possess enough Greek to undertake the complex and formidable task of transplanting a Greek play without also "colonializing" it or stripping it of its deep cultural difference, its remoteness from us. And that means depriving the play of that crucial *otherness* of Greek experience—a quality no less valuable to us than its closeness. Collaboration between scholar and poet is therefore the essential operating principle of the series. In fortunate cases scholar and poet co-exist; elsewhere we have teamed able poets and scholars in an effort to supply, through affinity and intimate collaboration, the necessary combination of skills.

An effort has been made to provide the general reader or student with first-rate critical introductions, clear expositions of translators' principles, commentary on difficult passages, ample stage directions, and glossaries of mythical terms encountered in the plays. Our purpose throughout has been to make the reading of the plays as vivid as possible. But our poets have constantly tried to remember that they were translating *plays*—plays meant to be produced, in language that actors could speak, naturally and with dignity. The poetry aims at being *dramatic* poetry and realizing itself in words and actions that are both speakable and playable.

Finally, the reader should perhaps be aware that no pains have been spared in order that the "minor" plays should be translated as carefully and

brilliantly as the acknowledged masterpieces. For the Greek Tragedy in
New Translations aims to be, in the fullest sense, *new*. If we need vigorous
new poetic versions, we also need to see the plays with fresh eyes, to reassess
the plays *for ourselves*, in terms of our own needs. This means translations
that liberate us from the canons of an earlier age because the translators
have recognized, and discovered, in often neglected works, the perceptions
and wisdom that make these works ours and necessary to us.

A NOTE ON THE SERIES FORMAT

If only for the illusion of coherence, a series of thirty-three Greek plays
requires a consistent format. Different translators, each with his individual
voice, cannot possibly develop the sense of a single coherent style for each
of the three tragedians; nor even the illusion that, despite their differences,
the tragedians share a common set of conventions and a generic, or period,
style. But they can at least share a common approach to orthography and a
common vocabulary of conventions.

1. Spelling of Greek Names

Adherence to the old convention whereby Greek names were first Latinized
before being housed in English is gradually disappearing. We are now
clearly moving away from Latinization and toward precise transliteration.
The break with tradition may be regrettable, but there is much to be said for
hearing and seeing Greek names as though they were both Greek and *new*,
instead of Roman or neo-classical importations. We cannot of course see
them as wholly new. For better or worse certain names and myths are too
deeply rooted in our literature and thought to be dislodged. To speak of
"Helene" and "Hekabe" would be no less pedantic and absurd than to write
"Aischylos" or "Platon" or "Thoukydides." There are of course borderline
cases. "Jocasta" (as opposed to "Iokaste") is not a major mythical figure in
her own right; her familiarity in her Latin form is a function of the fame of
Sophocles' play as the tragedy *par excellence*. And as tourists we go to
Delphi, not Delphoi. The precisely transliterated form may be pedantically
"right," but the pedantry goes against the grain of cultural habit and actual
usage.

As a general rule, we have therefore adopted a "mixed" orthography
according to the principles suggested above. When a name has been firmly
housed in English (admittedly the question of domestication is often moot),
the traditional spelling has been kept. Otherwise names have been transliterated. Throughout the series the *-os* termination of masculine names has
been adopted, and Greek diphthongs (as in Iphigen*ei*a) have normally been
retained. We cannot expect complete agreement from readers (or from

translators, for that matter) about borderline cases. But we want at least to make the operative principle clear: to walk a narrow line between orthographical extremes in the hope of keeping what should not, if possible, be lost; and refreshing, in however tenuous a way, the specific sound and name-boundedness of Greek experience.

2. Stage directions

The ancient manuscripts of the Greek plays do not supply stage directions (though the ancient commentators often provide information relevant to staging, delivery, "blocking," etc.). Hence stage directions must be inferred from words and situations and our knowledge of Greek theatrical conventions. At best this is a ticklish and uncertain procedure. But it is surely preferable that good stage directions should be provided by the translator than that the reader should be left to his own devices in visualizing action, gesture, and spectacle. Obviously the directions supplied should be both spare and defensible. Ancient tragedy was austere and "distanced" by means of masks, which means that the reader must not expect the detailed intimacy ("He shrugs and turns wearily away," "She speaks with deliberate slowness, as though to emphasize the point," etc.) which characterizes stage directions in modern naturalistic drama. Because Greek drama is highly rhetorical and stylized, the translator knows that his words must do the real work of inflection and nuance. Therefore every effort has been made to supply the visual and tonal sense required by a given scene and the reader's (or actor's) putative unfamiliarity with the ancient conventions.

3. Numbering of lines

For the convenience of the reader who may wish to check the English against the Greek text or vice versa, the lines have been numbered according to both the Greek text and the translation. The lines of the English translation have been numbered in multiples of ten, and these numbers have been set in the right-hand margin. The (inclusive) Greek numeration will be found bracketed at the top of the page. The reader will doubtless note that in many plays the English lines out-number the Greek, but he should not therefore conclude that the translator has been unduly prolix. In most cases the reason is simply that the translator has adopted the free-flowing norms of modern Anglo-American prosody, with its brief, breath-and emphasis-determined lines, and its habit of indicating cadence and caesuras by line length and setting rather than by conventional punctuation. Other translators have preferred four-beat or five-beat lines, and in these cases Greek and English numerations will tend to converge.

4. Notes and Glossary

In addition to the Introduction, each play has been supplemented by Notes (identified by the line numbers of the translation) and a Glossary. The Notes are meant to supply information which the translators deem important to the interpretation of a passage; they also afford the translator an opportunity to justify what he has done. The Glossary is intended to spare the reader the trouble of going elsewhere to look up mythical or geographical terms. The entries are not meant to be comprehensive; when a fuller explanation is needed, it will be found in the Notes.

Boston   WILLIAM ARROWSMITH AND HERBERT GOLDER

CONTENTS

SUPPLIANT WOMEN

INTRODUCTION

I COMPETING VIEWS

The story behind Euripides' *Suppliant Women* calls to mind global politics: a small and vulnerable country appeals to a major power to defend it against the barbarism of a tyrannical neighboring state. The *Suppliant Women,* which recalls a mythical event in Athenian prehistory, and one which gave the Athenians of the fifth and fourth centuries great pride, is just such a tale of three cities. In it, a helpless Argos, unable to recover her war dead fallen before the gates of Thebes, appeals to Athens for help. Driven by its defense of Greek religious law that all Hellenes, regardless of their sins, deserve burial, Athens agrees to intervene against Thebes on behalf of the dead. These disputed dead occupy the moral center of the play and, far from silent, will by the end of the drama even appear on stage.

While the Athenians of the classical period tended to look upon this benevolent and disinterested gesture as Athens' finest hour,[1] the question remains: Does Euripides echo that sentiment in his *Suppliant Women* (produced between 424 and 419 B.C.)? The Argument accompanying the play's manuscript says yes, calling this play "a praise of Athens." But the many jarring episodes and the unrelieved lament of the chorus in the last half of the play complicate such an easy interpretation. Responding to these and other episodes, many modern readers simply dismiss the play as flawed, its tone inconsistent, its structure incoherent, its scenes overblown.

The *Suppliant Women* has not benefited from the general modern admiration for Euripides' daring dramaturgy, characterized by contradictory voices and loosely linked, quickly shifting scenes. Euripides creates an

---

1. Cf. Herodotus, I.27; Lysias "Funeral Oration for the Men Who Supported the Corinthians" 7–10 (392 B.C., or later); Isocrates *Panegyricus* 54–58 (about 380 B.C.) and his *Panathenaicus* 168–74 (342 B.C.); Demosthenes "The Funeral Oration" 8 (perhaps 338 B.C.).

3

energetic but restless surface, fracturing single points of perspective, as in cubist art, offering no point of stability, leaving no position, once established, untested. If such craft in other Euripidean plays is admired, even envied, by modern sensibilities, here it is chastised.

But this general condemnation is, in my opinion, wrong. This is a masterful work, a dramatic poem of formidable power in its uncompromising juxtapositions of conflicting pulls on the human psyche. In the analysis which follows I hope to give some sense of its texture and movement as well as its moral passion.[2]

II DEMETER AND ATHENA: STRUCTURE AND TONE

Euripides' *Suppliant Women* is usually interpreted as a play of two parts. In the first, Argive supplication leads to war and Athenian recovery of the unburied dead (1–735);[3] in the second part, where the mothers mourn for the dead, the tone shifts abruptly as victory brings lament and brightness gives way to despair (736–1184). Although one can clearly divide the play in this way, concentration on that structure masks another ordering principle which is in *my* opinion of equal, or greater, weight. Like Euripides' *Hippolytus* of 428 B.C., which begins with a prologue by Aphrodite and draws to a close with Artemis as a *dea ex machina,* this play opens with the worship of one goddess and closes with the appearance of another from the *machina* (or perhaps *theologeion*). These goddesses of competing temperaments, Demeter and Athena, frame the play and contain, to some degree, the explosive internal movements.

As in the *Hippolytus,* the two framing deities, though not entirely absent, often seem invisible in the main body of the work and even extraneous to much of the argument about whether or not to support the suppliants. In that regard, we might say that the story is complete without the gods. But the divine "presence" at either end of that drama sets the foreground world of human activity and individual tragedy against a wider background of divine forces, placing the particular and seemingly idiosyncratic in the context of generic and universal forces (or divine beings personifying those universals). Presiding over the human story of supplication and retrieval of the dead, Demeter and Athena represent different and almost irreconcilable aspects of the world: one concerned with fertility, life, death, and

---

2. In recent years a number of critics have begun to reappraise this neglected gem. See Rush Rehm's *Greek Tragic Theatre* (London, 1992), 123–32, and his article "The Staging of Suppliant Plays," *Greek, Roman and Byzantine Studies* 29 (1988), 263–307; Peter Burian, "*Logos* and *Pathos:* The Politics of the *Suppliant Women,*" in *Directions in Euripidean Criticism,* ed. P. Burian (Durham, N.C., 1985), 129–55; Wesley Smith, "Expressive Form in Euripides' *Suppliants,*" *Harvard Studies in Classical Philology* 71 (1966), 151–70.

3. Line references refer to our translation unless otherwise indicated.

renewal; the other with political discourse, military action, and Realpolitik. As seldom as these realms intersect, there is a moment in the play when, in the figure of Aithra, they seem to merge.

Critics of this play rarely mention Demeter, no doubt in part because they are inclined to read rather than to see ancient tragedy. But the opening tableau of sacrifice at the altar to Demeter and Persephone at Eleusis is more than a convenience for the central plot. Aithra is honoring Demeter and her daughter at the annual Panhellenic festival in late October, called the Proerosia, for the first fruits of the year's harvest.

The staging of the opening scene calls attention to the festival. At our temporal and cultural distance from the original, we do not know if tragedy began with the entrance of the participants or at the first spoken words. But evidence in the text of the *Suppliant Women* suggests the following stage directions. Before any words are spoken, Aithra enters with temple attendants from the temple doors. They are robed in ceremonial white, appropriate for the rite they are about to perform. When Aithra moves to the orchestra to take her seat at the altar to Demeter and her daughter, the audience would expect the prologue to begin. But, in a gesture unique among all surviving tragedies, the chorus (fifteen women), accompanied by their own attendants, enter *in silence* from stage left (Thebes). In their company are Adrastos and the sons of the Dead. Adrastos interrupts Aithra as she is sacrificing—all this without words—and then turns with the sons to the stage near the temple doors. The mothers, dressed in dark "robes not meant for festival" (97 in the Greek) and with heads shorn in mourning, surround Aithra in a circle of suppliant boughs, in a manner "not reverent . . . but driven by need" (64–65). The interruption of Demeter's festival threatens to bring pollution on all of Attica. Only after this tableau does Aithra speak her prologue, explaining the significance of the actions which have just occurred. Like an overture before an opera, this pantomime before the prologue establishes potential tensions between the unfulfilled burial rites and the interrupted fertility rites, each rite making its own demands on the earth and the community.[4]

But in spite of the obvious contrast between worshipers and mourners, the Argive women and Demeter in her festival share points of common experience. Like the mourning women, Demeter is a mother who has suffered loss. But unlike her mortal counterparts, Demeter has lived through that grief to experience renewed life and restoration, both in the form of the "death" and rebirth of her daughter Persephone and in the form of nature's annual dying and renewal associated with the Proerosia. There

4. For an excellent account of this tableau, see Peter Burian, "The Play before the Prologue: Initial Tableaux on the Greek Stage," in *Ancient and Modern: Essays in Honor of Gerald Else,* ed. J. H. D'Arms and J. W. Eadie (Ann Arbor, Mich., 1977), 79–94.

is, then, an implicit harmony, as well as dissonance, between the fore-grounded mortal concern for retrieval of the unburied dead and the body's return to the earth (517–21), and the backgrounded "setting" of nature's renewal and Demeter's mysteries (cf. 174). Characteristic of Euripidean drama, a pattern ultimately joyous on the divine level will be experienced as grief by mortals.

The earth, invoked over and over in Aithra's opening, reveals how many different ways a single word can be interpreted in this play: earth as the source and nurse of life, as its final resting place, and in political terms as the "homeland of Argos" or the "land of Pittheus." A single concept opens up a whole panorama of oppositions that the play will explore, human and natural, male and female, political and religious. But here we need to concentrate on the first line of the play, "Demeter, hearth[*hestia*]-holder of the Eleusinian land" (in the Greek). Demeter's name not only begins the play but introduces a cluster of values significant throughout: earth and mother, soil and place, and a domestic orientation (*hestia*).

Athena will aggressively reorient such concerns at the play's end. Severely criticized by many readers for her inhumanity and for her demand of blood vengeance, Athena as Athena Polias informs Theseus that he must perform sacrifices to cement formal treaties between Athens and Argos and then bury the sacrificial knife in a corner of the earth (1157) near the burial mounds in Eleusis. If the Argives ever march against Athens, she informs him, this instrument will rise up out of the earth in vengeance. A far cry from Demeter's Proerosia, in Athena's political vision the earth's produce is a "biting knife" (1156), its harvest political, military, and bloodthirsty.

III MOTHER AND SON: AITHRA AND THESEUS

Aithra, who appears in the first third of *Suppliant Women,* is one of Euripides' greatest visionary characters. Like many women in Greek tragedy, she controls the movement of the scene of which she is a part. While the male figures from Argos (Adrastos and the sons of the Seven) are relegated to the stage in prone mourning positions, she dominates the theater from her seat in the orchestra at the altar, burning cakes of thanksgiving, "bound, but not bound, by (suppliant) boughs" (30–31). Both Aithra and the Proerosia festival appear to be Euripidean inventions in the story of Argive supplication of Theseus. In other versions of this myth, the Argive women supplicate Theseus directly or are silent as Adrastos speaks to Theseus on their behalf. By adding Aithra to the myth, Euripides is able to set up a contrast between an initial supplication between mothers and a subsequent one between two (male) heads of state, a distinction marked visually as one occurs in the orchestra, the other on stage. Aithra's immediate compassion for the mothers (gray-haired like her) and her reverence for their cause serve as foil for the failed supplication between Adrastos and Theseus. If Aithra responds to the mothers with a sense of religious urgency (she sends for her son, hoping that he will "discharge our obligation through some deed / the gods approve" [37–38]), Theseus responds to Adrastos with dispassionate, and then antagonistic, reasoned discourse. The juxtaposition of the two supplication scenes can be compared to the point and counterpoint of a fugue, as if the renewed supplication repeats the first exposition in a new key, now of male voices from the stage, expanding and opposing the established themes of female voices in the orchestra.[5]

The new tone is immediately evident when the young Athenian king turns to the aged Argive ruler: "Uncover your head, and stop those groans. / Nothing can be accomplished without speech" (112–13). For Theseus speech is a gift from the gods which, making the faculty of understanding possible, sets men (of the polis) apart from beasts. Speech for Theseus will take two forms: a rapid-fire interrogation as he tries to get to the bottom of things (Why did you attack Thebes? Did you have divine backing?), followed by a full-blown rhetorical confrontation wherein each protagonist delivers a speech constructed according to the standard rules of forensic argumentation.

In his debate, Theseus offers a theodicy (much criticized by modern scholars for its supposed irrelevance), in which he pontificates about a divinely benevolent and moral universe. Confident in this model of the cosmos, he lectures the older Adrastos on the realities of political conflict and good forms of government, fully aware that mortals must be on guard against those who (like Adrastos) think they "are wiser than all the gods" (219). Prudence requires that Theseus not support Adrastos in an alliance. At no time in his confrontation with Adrastos does Theseus acknowledge the suffering of the Argive mothers or the rights of the unburied dead. If the king's reasoning sounds pompous and irrelevant, as critics complain (but see commentary at 196–219), it is meant to. But only in part. There is something boyish about Theseus—on the verge of manhood, skilled in hunting boar but untried as a king—whose theories about government are still more abstract than tempered by experience.

This play will prove to be Theseus' coming of age, his battle initiation into manhood. In a pattern unique in the stories of extant tragedy, and almost unparalleled in the surviving stories of Greek mythology, his mother will be the one to show him the way. Though Theseus had been unmoved by a direct choral supplication (when the chorus moved temporarily to the

---

5. For a fine application of this analogy to Euripidean dramaturgy, see Anne Michelini, *Euripides and the Tragic Tradition* (Madison, Wis., 1987), 119; see also Cedric Whitman, *Euripides and the Full Circle of Myth* (Cambridge, Mass., 1974), 113.

stage [272–83]), he is taken aback by his mother's wails and tears (289–90). As a woman, Aithra is reluctant to interfere in the affairs of state, as she herself says, but, compelled by her sense of what is good and noble (*kalon*), she can no longer hold back. In one of the great speeches of the play mediating the antitheses of the opening scene—emotional versus rational, personal versus political, female versus male, old versus young—Aithra redefines Theseus' sense of what it means to be a hero, a king, a citizen of Athens, and a member of the whole Panhellenic community.

Her words deserve close scrutiny. Afraid that her son has tripped up (*sphallei* [300]), no less than Adrastos did when he helped Polynices (see also 157), Aithra first speaks of religious matters, correcting and expanding her son's understanding of gods and law: "My son, first and foremost, it's the will of the gods / you have to consider" (298–99). Theseus' theodicy is deficient in at least one respect: honor demands that he stop "those bandits who confound the sacred laws / of all Greece [*nomima pasēs Hellados*]. All civilized order rests / on this; the safekeeping of laws [*nomoi*]" (308–10). This larger appeal is cast within a personal and civic one. Dismissing her own maternal fears, Aithra tells Theseus that it is time for him to move from adolescent, and Heraclean heroics—the hunting of wild boars, "a trifling labor" or sport, as Aithra calls it (*phaulos ponos* [313])—to manly ones. Aithra's vision of true heroism binds personal identity ("My son, if you are indeed / my son, don't shame yourself" [316–17]) and personal honor (303) with civic action and civic glory ("you wouldn't want it said that you hung back, / afraid, when you could have wrested the crown / of fame for the city" [311–13]). Under the pressure of her language, heroic *ponos* is fused with civic *ponos*: "In her labors (*ponoi*)," Aithra exclaims, "[Athens] soars in strength and pride" [320].

Challenged by his mother, Theseus defends his reasoning and judgment against Adrastos (330–32), but accepts Aithra's larger vision: "I cannot shun this labor [*ponos*]. / What would my enemies say of me if you, / who gave me birth and who still fear for me, / are the first to bid me to take up such labor [*ponos*]? / I'll do it" (338–42). Personal and state duties formally converge when Theseus announces upon his return from Athens that the people of his city were "more than pleased to accept this labor" (*ponos* [389]).

Adrastos, we hear in the prologue, asked Aithra to make the work (of burial) common to Theseus and Athens (26–27). Like *ponos*, the word *koinon* (common) is important in the play as it joins the communal lament of the grievers, the shared burden of burial, and the equalizing experience of Hades to the laws which are common to all those within a city (415, 423) as well as to those linking states (523). It is just such a fusion that Aithra achieves through her compassion and understanding of an enlightened heroism, joining people and perspectives that earlier seemed to have little in common. Theseus' move down off the stage into the orchestra to join hands with his mother visually symbolizes Aithra's success in fulfilling Adrastos' wish. The "soprano" and "tenor" voices, as it were, competing contrapuntally from the orchestra and the stage, appear at this point to have achieved unexpected harmony. The force of this tragedy, however, will be that, despite Aithra's character and Theseus' personal maturation (still to be seen in full), the discovery of "common ground" will fail.

IV THESEUS: WORD AND SPEAR

After Aithra's speech and Theseus' change of heart, we witness a new harmony of views, as chorus and actors, orchestra and stage appear to share a common language and common goals (361–735). So the mothers sing of *eusebēs ponos* (holy labor), "[which] brings an honored prize / to our cities, and gratitude [*kharis*] / "forever" (369–71), and they adjure Theseus to "Take care: don't stain the laws / of mortals" (374–75). One mark of this harmony is the greatly reduced role of the chorus over these four hundred lines. There are only two odes in this section, and the first is among the shortest in all Greek tragedy (361–76). Both serve to provide space between related events: the first allows Theseus to leave for Athens to consult with the people (*dēmos*) and muster an army; the second acts as a bridge between Theseus setting out for war against Thebes and the news of his victory (578–607). The "bridge" effect of these songs conveys the sense of a seamless flow of events as the mothers and the city work toward a common end.

Echoing his earlier debate with Adrastos, Theseus in the second episode enters into a struggle of words (421) with an older herald from Thebes. Euripides surely pokes fun at the young king's compulsive need to argue with his seniors, even when as here his elder is a "clever herald" from the enemy camp. But behind that fun is a more serious note, revealed in part by the reverse order of the new argument as compared to the first debate. Whereas the first "contest" proceeded from cross-examination to sustained set pieces and eventual successful persuasion, this confrontation begins with formal debate and degenerates into one-line exchanges, anger, and insult. The self-conscious repetition and reversal are deliberate, designed to reveal the inability of words to settle certain hostilities. Euripides makes the point yet again when Athens, with its army before the Cadmean Gates, tries a second time to persuade by diplomacy rather than by war. Creon responds in silence, perhaps the most articulate marker of language's impotence to settle disputes between states. Athena's impatience with verbal promises at the end of the play, though much criticized by later readers, surely derives from a superior wisdom about the power of language to control military passion.

Theseus' debate with the Theban Herald about the relative merits of democracy and tyranny (394–452), has also been criticized as dramatically
irrelevant. Far from irrelevant, the debate displays before our eyes that in a
democracy small men enjoy equal footing with the rich and powerful. In
Theseus' words: "when a wealthy citizen does wrong, / a weaker one can
criticize, and prevail, / with justice on his side. *That's* liberty" (427–29).
This characteristic of an idealized Athens is crucial for the city and to the
play itself as we have witnessed a woman, not even a citizen, unable to keep
silent, change the course of Athenian history and the narrow view of its
leading figure. When the Theban Herald echoes Theseus' earlier sentiment that it would be impious to help those who are themselves impious
(483–93; cf. 158, 229–31), the Athenian ruler answers by repeating the
lesson he has learned from Aithra. But in so doing he expands upon the
reasons his mother had so succinctly given (cf. 504–45 to 298–327, esp.
512–26 to 308–10) and reveals in that "repetition" a new and broader
awareness of his own humanity: "Now, let the corpses be hidden in the
earth / from which each came to light; let soul release / to air, body to earth.
We do not own / our bodies, but are mere tenants there for life, / and earth
that nursed them takes them back again" (517–21). Not only has Theseus
learned from Aithra, but he seems to have gained an insight into the
rhythms implicit in Demeter's festival itself. Far from being irrelevant,
Theseus' theorizing sets the Demeter themes into a new political context
and shows in the *agōn* of debate how the ideal city balances the claims of
the living and the dead.

But it is equally crucial to realize that this debate is not an unabashed
praise of Athens. The Herald's questions about democracy's vulnerability
are never fully refuted. At the time of this play, demagogues in Athens did,
as the Herald says literally in the Greek, "puff up the citizens by words"
(405). With new self-made leaders like the leather merchant Cleon, the
rope seller Eucrates, and the lamp maker Hyperbolus, the Herald's words
have bite: "it's a disease, when, fresh / from his ditch, some dirt farmer
bridles the mob / and drives it with the witchery of his tongue" (416–18).
Theseus' quip, "Well, what a clever herald!" (419) is funny but feeble. His
taunt that the Thebans have little to fear from the buried dead ("Can
children in earth's womb / beget revenge?" [529–30]) is equally insufficient
and will be refuted by the play's end.

The Herald's fear that all Greece is mad for war (474) is even more
significant. If he as an emissary from unjust Thebes is easy to dismiss,
his words are not. When, later in the play, Adrastos grieves at the sight
of the retrieved corpses and cries out for peace, we cannot but be deeply
moved:

> Tormented race of man,
> why do you take up spears, and bring down death
> upon each other? Stop! Leave off those labors,
> guard your city in peace. The needs of life
> are small. You should provide for them
> gently, without such gruesome labor.
>
> (904–9)

The heroic labors (*ponoi*) which Aithra encouraged, Adrastos here denounces. Civic action is suddenly less glorious when seen in the face of personal anguish; positions once thought noble are rephrased in a different key. Such juxtaposition vibrates at the heart of Euripides' contrapuntal art and it is to his credit that he does not try to soften, or resolve, the strain of competing values.

Tested in war, Theseus has proven himself every bit the hero in a civic cause and with civic moderation. Not only does he win the day but, just as impressively, he exhibits self-restraint in victory. But if Adrastos responds to war with a new pacifism, the experience of battle has transformed Theseus in a different way—the sententious and neophyte king has been humanly touched by war and by death "common" to all (760). Far from the figure who said to Aithra "You shouldn't suffer their grief" (289), Theseus, washed like the other combatants in "rivers of blood" (658), feels an affection (*ēgapa* [728]) for the war dead whose bodies he washes with his own hands and prepares for cremation. The verb (*agapaō*), found only in Euripides among the tragic poets and only in the context of loved ones caring for the corpses of nearest kin (a father for a son's body, a wife for a husband's), testifies to the bond of kinship Theseus feels for the dead.

When not performed by family members, the washing of the wounds and cremation of the body are normally associated with slaves, as Adrastos says in the Greek a "bitter" labor even for them (724). Few critics seem to have appreciated the full force of this passage. Adrastos says such work would be "a terrible burden and shame" (730) for Theseus. But for the young man the experience of battle appears to have obliterated class distinctions, so king and slave are one and the same, and the common lot makes us all a "family." By calling these tasks that Theseus undertakes for the dead a labor (*ponos* [725, 893]), Euripides continues to examine and redefine the meaning of this word. Confined neither to the trifling *ponos* of boar hunts nor to the civic labor of this war, in this new usage *ponos* joins, or makes common, hero and slave. That grounding of the heroic in the necessities of mortality is not unlike war itself with its "dust storming up to heaven" (656).

V VICTORY AND LAMENT

Even this unique form of "heroism" proves unstable and short-lived. In the last third of the drama, where the rituals of mourning are reenacted step by step, changes in mood are sudden and sharp and the meanings of words shift abruptly. Exposing the contradictory emotions associated with public funerals, the *Suppliant Women* juxtaposes savage grief with civic eulogy, old with young, personal pain with forms of "heroism." In response to the Athenian recovery of their sons, the Argive women lament: "My joys woven with sorrow" (742). If glorious for Athens (743–45), for the chorus of mothers to look upon "my sons' corpse" is a "horror and beauty—/ longed-for, unhoped-for day, / seen at last, greatest in tears" (745–48) (the use of the first-person singular intensifies the sense of pain felt individually). Demeter-like in her despair at the loss of a child, each mother grieves over the "children torn from my arms" (756).

The outpouring of grief intensifies when Adrastos brings out the bodies. Though most commentators argue that he leaves the bodies in the orchestra, the pathos of the scene is increased, as we shall see, if they are carried to the stage in sight of the mothers but beyond their reach. The *kommos,* or lyric exchange, between an actor and the chorus (and between orchestra and stage [757–96]) expresses the pain that binds the two areas of the theater together. In this scene, tragedy verges toward opera and discourse toward song as sounds frequently break beyond the boundaries of coherent speech. Fifteen choral members with seven children of the dead in the orchestra and Adrastos on stage with ten (or fourteen) Athenian pallbearers carrying five biers, close to forty people in all, make up this spectacle in one of Euripides' most elaborate theatrical displays. A cry that Adrastos begins (on stage), the chorus ends (in the orchestra) (e.g., ADRASTOS: *iō, iō* CHORUS: *tōn g'emōn egō* [768]; ADRASTOS: *epathomen, ō* . . . CHORUS: *ta kuntat'algē kakōn* [770]). The call and response between king and chorus allow for a harmony in grief but it is one which will be shattered by a new dissonance.

The tone of the mourning changes with Theseus' reentry as the king transforms remembrance of the dead from dirge to eulogy. Though patient while the Argive mothers and Adrastos grieve, he wants Adrastos to use the moment for civic objectives, seeing in the funeral an opportunity for teaching young citizens lessons in the meaning of virtue and (military) excellence. Delivering an encomium, Adrastos concludes this oration with the following maxim: "Noble upbringing begets nobility / . . . high courage [*euandria*] / can be taught, just as a babe is taught / to speak and listen to things he doesn't know" (865–69). How can we understand these long periodic sentences, in their measured cadences and praise of reasoned speech, coming from a man who moments before was unable to utter even articulate sounds? How are we to reconcile this Adrastos with the man who recently concluded from Athens' victory that man lacks even the power of thought (700–701)? Both before and after the funeral oration Adrastos laments that a wiser race would use reason, not the sword, to resolve differences (710–13, 905–9). Does Euripides mean for us to read the teachability of courage ironically? The irony seems most apparent when the Argive dead are expressly praised for the qualities they expressly lacked. In particular, Capaneus, hubristic and justly avenged by Zeus as the Herald (484–89) and the chorus (499–500) have already said earlier in the play, is now praised for moderation: "He set his sights / no higher than a poor man" (821–22). How do we reconcile such obvious contradictions within the play? Poor craftsmanship or deliberate strategy? The praise seems stereotypic, as if the occasion of public remembrance, rather than fact, determines language. The obvious discrepancy between truth and funerary rhetoric in the case of the Argive heroes shows vividly how public praise absorbs the dead to civic need, and, as in the earlier, discordant versions of democracy, reveals discrepancy between the ideal and the actual as part of the play's structure.

The surprising transition from *kommos* to public funeral oration may again be understood as a fuguelike interplay of voice and counter voice, showing paradoxical perspectives of the living toward the war dead. Rather than being disingenuous, Adrastos' change of mood from lyric grief to public praise reveals how one in mourning tries "not unwillingly" (817, literal translation) to find something uplifting, ennobling, inspirational in pain. While we sense irony in the gulf between the actual deeds of the dead and the clichés designed to instruct the living, there is an even greater irony in the clash between public need and personal grief. That tension Euripides explores for the remainder of the play.

As soon as Adrastos finishes his oration with the maxim quoted above, the mothers sing a short, but powerful, iambic strophe of seven lines (872–78). Oblivious to the words of public praise, they force us to see the dead again in terms of personal and maternal loss. Echoing their earlier invocations of the labors of birth and loss (86), they refer to the pains of childbirth as labors (*ponoi*) and hardship (*mokhthon athlias*) (876–77), and further force us to see a woman's world as an alternative heroism centered around an identity with the house and procreation rather than with military courage and city glory. Medea, in Euripides' play of the same name (431 B.C.), similarly suggests that the labors of childbirth—and the female role in the house—greatly exceed the dangers (and values) of conventional Greek views of heroism: "Men say of us that we have a peaceful time living at home, while they go to war. How wrong they are! I would much rather stand three times in the front of battle than bear one child" (248–51).

Theseus speaks next, picking up where Adrastos left off, as if the choral interlude had not occurred. The beginning of his recitation, "and further-more" (*kai mēn* [925] in the Greek), makes a smooth transition from Adrastos' praise of the five whose bodies have been recovered and Theseus' remembrance of Amphiaraos and Polynices. This is orchestration at its best: the male voices from the stage in measured iambic trimeters, the mothers' voices from the orchestra in quickened, often abbreviated iambic dimeters.

Before the funeral oration, the mothers had asked to embrace their sons, a request that Adrastos appeared to have granted (777–79). Apparently they never reached, or touched, the corpses on stage as is evident when Adrastos over a hundred lines later says to the chorus: "Go, bereaved mothers, approach your children" (895). Without warning or compromise, Theseus prevents this long-awaited contact. Shocked, Adrastos asks: "What do you mean? Shouldn't mothers touch their children?" (897). But he then backs down: to Theseus, "you win" (literally translated); to the chorus, "Be brave, and stay there. / Theseus is right. When they've burned on the pyre, / you can embrace their bones" (901–3). Theseus has appropriated the women's cultural right for himself and for the city, personally washing the bodies of the dead and requesting that the mourning of the dead serve a civic pur-pose.[6] Are we to understand his rationale ("[The mothers] would die, seeing the mutilation" [898]) as a civic desire to curtail the impassioned and disorderly laments of women and the house (*oikos*)? I think so. In concert with his other actions, Theseus' prohibition appears as an attempt to define kinship civically and to suppress personal cries of pain with a more verbally self-controlled, pedagogic mourning ritual. The competition between voices is becoming more focused, exposing a deep-seated cultural struggle between the competing claims of city and house, male and female. If I am right, that polyphony is visually accentuated when the mothers about to mount the stairs to the stage are abruptly stopped by Theseus. Aithra's union of reason and emotion, city and family is a thing of the past as public and private grief pull in different directions.

The next episode—among the most daring and experimental in the entire Euripidean repertoire for its complete liberty from legendary mate-rial, its raw emotionality, its unannounced introduction of new characters, its fresh development ("inadequately motivated," critics moan)—is linked to the preceding ode by meter and theme. Bride of the hubristic Capaneus

---

6. Nicole Loraux sees a further appropriation, in the Athenian State Theater taking over the song-making traditions of lamentation; see *Les Mères en deuil* (Paris, 1990).

and the daughter of Iphis, Evadne enters from a cliff overhanging Eleusis high above the stage. Dressed in wedding clothes, she reveals in an arialike monody (in Aeolics, like the previous ode) that she intends to leap from the cliff into her husband's pyre. As the song draws to a close, Iphis rushes in from Argos, searching for his daughter. In front of her father's eyes, indifferent to his pleas, Evadne leaps to her death (into Capaneus' pyre), making this and Ajax's suicide in Sophocles' play the only deaths "seen" by an audience in Greek tragedy.

But how successful is the experiment? Thematic concerns motivate the scene. By exclusively focusing on the family and introducing a fresh death, the scene clearly revives and expands the theme of parental anguish. The collective pain of the mothers is concentrated on a single person; parental grief, conventionally expressed by women, finds a male voice. Like the mothers, Iphis claims that if he had it to do over again, he would have neither a son (Eteoklos, killed at Thebes) nor a daughter. Now in this play both mothers and a father look forward only to death.

Seeing her suicide as a marriage, Evadne asserts that she is going to join her husband in Persephone's marriage chambers (translated literally) (973), a union she imagines with erotic anticipation: "melting in radiant flame, / my body will mingle with yours, . . . loved husband, flesh to flesh" (970–72; cf. 960–61, 1023). The word translated as marriage chamber (*thalamos*) can equally well mean funeral chamber, as it does elsewhere in Euripides, easily joining themes of marriage and death in Evadne's mind. Evadne's reference to Persephone's marriage further evokes, rather parodies, the Demeter/Persephone story: the daughter desires marriage and actual death rather than life with her parent, and the daughter is oblivious to parental pain.

The Evadne story also reverses the family pattern in the opening scenes in which a mother, appealing to reason and an enlightened sense of human suffering, was able to prevent a son from wrongheaded action. Evadne, probably played by the Theseus actor (while Iphis is most likely played by the Adrastos actor), subverts, or perverts, and parodies much that Theseus has come to symbolize: contrary to the king's contest of words, Evadne engages in a prolonged, self-absorbed monologue; she speaks in a "riddle" (1016) rather than in language (translated literally) "that makes the faculty of reason possible" (204); contrary to Theseus, she has little desire to understand or to be understood by Iphis ("My plans would anger you if you heard them, / so I can't tell you, Father" [1002–3]). Most perverted is Evadne's sense of heroism. Life, rather than action, is laborious for her (*ponos* [957]). Her death leap is "for glory" (*eukleia* [967]); she claims a glorious triumph in coming to Eleusis (*kallinikos* [1011]; the word echoes Adrastos' invocation of Theseus at 114); dying with her husband is an act of excellence (*aretē* [1015]). Such language more properly evokes memory of Homeric heroes on the battlefield or Theseus' courage at Thebes. If the chorus move toward a heroism contrary to that of male values, this female imitation of a male heroism is narcissistic rather than ennobling, self-absorbed rather than altruistic in its self-sacrifice. As with the funeral oration, the disparity between true heroism and the rhetoric of heroism is deeply unsettling.

Evadne's position high above the stage visually testifies to her detachment from human sensibilities; the distance between her and Iphis down below (probably in the orchestra) accents the gulf between them. Contrary to the union of Theseus and Aithra, symbolized by the touching of hands, Evadne in farewell to her father says: "It's useless. You . . . can't take my hand" (1021). While her manic wrenching of the heroic ideal cannot undo the significance of Theseus' achievements and nobility of soul, her actions do force us to question the cost in human terms of all acts of glory. We cannot help but ask whether Adrastos was not right that humankind should strive for a life—short as it is—of peace, free from strife (905–10).

Sustaining the intensity from the last episode, the ashes of the dead, cremated during the Evadne/Iphis scene, are carried into the theater and onto the stage. Imitating the first *kommos* between Adrastos and the mothers, the sons of the Seven (silent throughout the play until this moment) and the mothers lament over their loved ones (in the play's final *kommos* [1065–1116], where iambics are used again); once more, the male voices come from the stage, the female from the orchestra, but the repetition is designed to point up difference. When the corpses first appeared, the aged Adrastos and the gray-haired mothers joined in a common grief; but the ashes stimulate extreme responses, diametrically opposed. Though the text here is quite corrupt in places, the general shape of the scene is reasonably clear.

Worn down by grief, the mothers praise pacifism (1099–1101). By the play's end they abandon their earlier interest in civic *ponos* and *kharis* (369–71), now imagining alternative and specifically female meanings for these words of war and heroism. Remembering their breast-feeding and maternal sleepless nights, they ask (translated literally): "Where is my burden [*ponos*] of children? where is the reward [*kharis*] of childbirth?" (1086–87). The sons of the Seven, on the other hand, oblivious to this female language, aspire to an ancient, even ancestral, form of virtue: "Father, do you hear your children mourn?/Will I ever avenge your death with my own shield?/May that day come for your child" (1094–96). The sons' prolonged silence so dramatically broken after a thousand lines is Aeschylean in technique, and chilling. At the end of the play, the young speak for the first time only to clarify and deepen the tragic themes of the play as

Adrastos' foolhardy war leads to further senseless war. The new voices confirm that the living have every cause to fear the power of the dead. As the Herald feared, a madness for war, not reason, is in the Greek blood. The sons, unquestionably, show that for Euripides the legend exposes the permanent impulse toward aggression and revenge and the fragility of calls for peace and renewal. The sons, and not the weary mothers, will "hold their noble fathers' bodies / in both hands" (1118; cf. 1075). The language of orchestra and stage could not be further apart.

VI COMPETING CLOSURES

This is a play of apparent resolutions and deep irresolution. In a short farewell between Theseus and Adrastos, harmony again appears to be restored as the play seems to conclude. The Athenian king ends by saying that the Argives "must *remember* these acts of kindness [*kharis*]," passing on "from son to son . . . these same words . . . to honor our city, enjoining them to remember what you have obtained from me. Zeus and the gods above are witness" (translated literally) (1121–27; emphasis added). Acknowledging Athenian beneficence and nobility, the Argive leader in return promises "undying thanks" (*kharis* again [1130]). *Kharis* has been restored to its political sense. Everlasting memory has been requested and promised. Words have been trusted to seal the bond. Zeus has been invoked as witness. Assuming the play is over—bodies recovered, cremations performed, gratitude expressed—the principals, chorus, and many mutes start to move toward the two exits.

But any sense of resolution is lost when Athena, appearing abruptly from high above the stage, halts the exodus. Her intervention is swift and impatient: "Listen, Theseus, to Athena's words" (1135). Although this epiphany is criticized by many as harsh and unnecessary, it is crucial to the play both formally and thematically. In a world where words have shifting meanings and in which emotions for revenge are no less strong than cries for peaceful coexistence, Athena has little tolerance for verbal promises of gratitude. She demands an alliance with Argos which is anchored by sworn oaths, sacrificial blood, and sacred relics, not verbal avowals of *kharis*. A tripod, not words, will serve as physical *reminder* (1155). She further demands a written record, not verbal memory; a tripod in Apollo's shrine at Delphi, not an invocation of Zeus, as divine witness. Remote and indifferent to human suffering (not unlike Evadne), Athena reminds us of the stern laws of a political reality. In her world, civic order demands that mutable words be made fast in bronze and infused with divinity (Apollo's shrine and sacrificial blood).

For the second time in the play, Theseus has been rebuked by a woman. In both instances, he acquiesces, but here the goddess is criticized by many as being "repulsive" for vindicating vengeance, or as being reprehensible for debasing Theseus' generous altruism and enlightened humanism, or as being "morally inferior to men" showing that the gods are neither "just" nor "kindly." But when were the ancient gods ever (simply) just or kindly? If less sensitive than humans to suffering, Athena bestows a divine form upon the grim and uncompromising realities of war and civic order. She is the necessary complement to Demeter and the pacific spirit that takes shape in *Suppliant Women.* As in *Hippolytus,* human beings are torn by competing goddesses who impose conflicting necessities on the human psyche.

Not a play of sublime language, and neither Aeschylean nor Sophoclean in lyric density, Euripides' *Suppliant Women* is a play of uncompromising force; in a sense its very refusal of poetic embellishment constitutes its peculiar power. Euripides' refusal to resolve competing claims upon the human psyche makes this a particularly painful work. Neither Athena nor Demeter prevails as the play tests the shifting weights of words and contradictory pulls upon our public and private selves. The *Suppliant Women* may rightly be criticized for its endless twists and reversals which could prove difficult to present on the modern stage. The multiple arenas of the Greek theater (orchestra, stage, and elevated "roof"), all used in the play, could, however, define spatially and render visually the drama's themes and variations. And at the heart of the play, magnetizing all language and gesture, lie the dead, whose speechless eloquence still makes claims on the living.

VII THE DATING OF EURIPIDES' *SUPPLIANT WOMEN*

In lieu of external evidence, the dating of the play depends on the discovery of possible historical allusions within the play and comparative stylistic analysis with other Euripidean dramas. Both pieces of evidence suggest a date between 424 and 419 B.C.

Possible historical allusions: in victory after the battle of Delium in November 424 B.C., Thebes refused to return the bodies of Athenian war dead for burial. In July 420 B.C., Athens and Argos formed a hundred-year alliance (cf. Thucy. 5.47, 5.82). Critics have argued that one, or both, of these events are alluded to in this play. We need to be leery, however, about making simple equivalences between the play and current events. The one-sided Argive indebtedness to Athens in the play hardly corresponds to the treaty agreements of 420 B.C. Similarities in the language of the historical treaty and Athena's demands for a formal alliance at the end of the play may suggest nothing more than Euripides' careful imitation of the conventions of diplomatic terminology. So it would be wrong to conclude that Euripides must be copying from the treaty or that he is arguing for the creation of such a treaty, although both theories have been proposed. It has also been argued that Euripides echoes dissenting political slogans circa 424–21 B.C. When considering the date of the play, the Athenian reorganization and revitalization of the Proerosia festival at Eleusis circa 420 B.C. should not be ignored,[7] and it is with this revival in mind that we prefer a production date circa 420. (For the Proerosia, see commentary *ad* 27–30.)

Comparative stylistic analysis of Euripidean metrical practices suggests that *Suppliant Women* comes from roughly the same period as his *Hecuba*, which can be dated no later than 423 B.C.

VIII THE TEXT

Euripides' *Suppliant Women* has benefited greatly from recent textual criticism and commentary, in particular from a fine edition of the play by Christopher Collard, *Euripides, Supplices* (Leipzig, 1984), itself improved by the careful work of James Diggle in his *Euripidis, Fabulae II* (Oxford, 1981) and its compendium, *Studies on the Text of Euripides* (Oxford, 1981). Collard also produced a commentary (and text) of very high quality: *Euripides, Supplices,* 2 vols. (Groningen, Neth., 1975). We are indebted to all these works; unless otherwise noted in the commentary, our translation is based on Collard's text of 1984.

Boston   S. S.
April 1994

We are grateful to Derek Walcott's Poets' Theatre in Boston and to Qwirk Productions, directed by Peter Dalto in New York City, for dramatized workshop readings of this play. We are also indebted to Rush Rehm for his two 1993 productions of the play, one at Stanford University, Stanford, California, and the other at The Folger Library in Washington, D.C.

Needham, Mass.   R. W. and S. S.
August 1994

7. See *Inscriptiones Graecae* I, 2nd ed., 76. Proposed dates for this inscription range from 423/22–419/18 B.C. For a translation of its key passages, see W. Burkert, *Greek Religion,* trans. J. Raffan (Cambridge, Mass., 1985), 67–68. See also H. W. Parke, *Festivals of the Athenians* (Ithaca, N.Y., 1977), 73–75.

SUPPLIANT WOMEN

CHARACTERS

AITHRA mother of Theseus

CHORUS mothers of the Seven "Argive" Dead who fought against Thebes

THESEUS king of Athens

ADRASTOS king of Argos, leader of the Seven against Thebes

HERALD a Theban

MESSENGER an Argive, reporting from Thebes

EVADNE an Argive; widow of Capaneus, one of the Seven; daughter of one of the mothers in the chorus; sister of Eteoklos, also of the Seven

IPHIS Evadne's father, an Argive

CHILDREN sons of the Seven

ATHENA protecting deity of Athens

Argive handmaidens; Temple priests; Athenian herald; Athenian pallbearers

Line numbers in the right-hand margin of the text refer to the English translation only, and references to the text in the notes at p. 65 are keyed to these lines unless otherwise specified. The bracketed line numbers in the running head lines refer to the Greek text. In the left-hand margin, "STR" refers to strophe and "ANT" to antistrophe, with no abbreviation for epode.

The scene is Demeter's temple at Eleusis, where Aithra has come to celebrate the Proerosia, an annual ritual held in late October where preliminary sacrifices are offered up for the land's tillage. In the orchestra, wearing ceremonial white, Aithra sits at an altar to Demeter and Kore and burns cake offerings. Demeter's priests stand in the background; the whole ensemble is surrounded by a chorus of women in black mourning clothes, holding suppliant boughs. On the stage, the sons of the Dead surround Adrastos, who lies prostrate in front of the temple doors.

AITHRA: Demeter, hearth goddess, guarding here
this land Eleusis, and you, her priests, now bless
me, bless Theseus my son, our city
Athens, and the land of Pittheus,
where my father raised me in a noble house
and married me to Aigeus, Pandion's son,
as Apollo willed.
     Even while I prayed
I looked on these old women here. They left
their homeland, Argos, and stunned by grief on grief
traveled with suppliant boughs to fall   10
at my knee. They have lost their children:
seven princely sons lie dead
by the gates of Thebes. Adrastos, King
of Argos, led them there, eager to win
a share of Oedipus' power for Polynices,
his exiled son-in-law.
       These mothers wish
to lay in the Earth the corpses of their sons,
but the rulers of Thebes, spiting the gods' laws,
refuse to let them gather up their dead.
Sharing the heaviness of their need for me   20
Adrastos lies, right here, eyes wet with tears
for the war and that doomed troop
he led from home. He urges me
to beg Theseus to rescue the dead
for sacred burial, by persuasion or by the spear.
He entrusts this task in common to my son
and to our city, Athens.
       I was just now
burning gifts for the fresh-plowed land: I came
from home to this shrine where the wheat

23

first pushes its bristling shoots above the earth.   30
Bound, but not bound, by boughs, I wait
here by the altars of the goddesses
Kore and Demeter. I am touched by these graying
mothers, cut from their sons: I honor their wreaths.

My herald has gone to Athens, calling Theseus
to free our land of their laments, or else
discharge our obligation through some deed
the gods approve. A wise woman
works most wisely through a man.

CHORUS

STR Old woman, I beg your help,   40
     falling at your knee,
      my voice harsh now with age.
Set my children free
     from lawless men who leave
      bodies, sodden in death, flung
as food for mountain beasts.

ANT Look, you see my eyes
     swollen, sluiced with tears,
      my gray and wrinkled flesh
shredded by my own hands. Why?   50
     Because I did not lay out
      my own dead son at home,
cannot see his grave in our Earth.

STR You gave birth yourself, once, Queen,
     to a boy who made your husband
      rejoice in the marriage bed. Join
your thought with mine, and share
     this grief I bear
      for the dead I brought from my womb.
I ask you, have your son   60
     go to Ismenus, bring back
      to my arms my son's strong body
     shamed, unburied, defiled.

ANT Not reverent, I come, but driven
          by need, falling forward, entreating,
          I intrude on these altars.
      My claims are righteous, and you,
          blessed with child, have power
          to heal my sorrow. I beg,
      let your living son place in my hands   70
          a corpse, let me cradle
          my poor dead child.

                              Addresses female attendants.

STR Now wail struggles with wail,
          servant girls clap hands and call.
      Come, beat breasts in time,
          come, share in our hymn,
          dance the dance Death loves.
      Furrow nails in white
          cheek, bring blood: cry out!
          Grief is the debt of grace we pay the dead.   80

ANT Joy of weeping, insatiable, thrusts me on
          in pain, as spring-water frets
      down the cliff face, high,
          unendingly, ever in tears.
          For woman, the child's death begets
      labor pains of lament:
          let me bury
      my sorrow, and die.

              Enter THESEUS, *into the orchestra, from the right.*

THESEUS: What's all this groaning, breast-beating, cries
          mourning the dead? The temples ring with echoes.   90
          I've rushed here, fearing: what if
          Mother, who left the house long back,
          has met some danger?
                          What in God's name?—Why is my mother
          sitting at the altar, an old woman surrounded by women,

strangers, with disorderly signs
of grief: old eyes driving tears
to Earth, butchered hair, black robes?
          Mother, what
is going on here? Speak up—
What in the world does this mean?   100

AITHRA: Child, these are the women whose sons—
the seven generals—died at the gates of Thebes.
See, my son: they guard me here
in their circle of suppliant boughs.

THESEUS: And this man, groaning at the door?

AITHRA: Adrastos, they call him, King of Argos.

THESEUS: And these boys around him? The women's sons?

AITHRA: No. The sons of the men who died.

THESEUS: What are they doing *here* with suppliant boughs?

AITHRA: Let them speak for themselves, my child.   110

                                        THESEUS *moves to the stage.*

THESEUS: You there, draped in that shawl.
Uncover your head, and stop those groans.
Nothing can be accomplished without speech.

ADRASTOS: Theseus, glorious in victory,
Lord of Athens, I come to you and your city,
a suppliant.

THESEUS: What is it? What do you ask?

ADRASTOS: You've heard of that army I led and lost?

THESEUS: You hardly marched through Greece in silence.

26

ADRASTOS: I destroyed my men, the finest of Argos.

THESEUS: Those are the wages of war.   120

ADRASTOS: I went to Thebes, asking for our dead.

THESEUS: So you could bury them properly?

ADRASTOS: Yes, but the Theban killers wouldn't allow it.

THESEUS: What did they say? Your request was sacred.

ADRASTOS: Since when has victory made men wise?

THESEUS: You want my advice? Or something more?

ADRASTOS: More, Theseus. To rescue the lost sons of Argos.

THESEUS: What about Argos? Were her boasts so empty?

ADRASTOS: We've fallen. We've come to you.

THESEUS: Is this your idea, or the whole city's?   130

ADRASTOS: All Argives beg you to bury the dead.

THESEUS: Why did you lead your seven troops against Thebes?

ADRASTOS: To help my two sons-in-law.

THESEUS: Which men of Argos did you choose for your daughters?

ADRASTOS: No Argive joined our house.

THESEUS: You married your girls to foreigners?

ADRASTOS: To Tydeus, and to Polynices the Theban.

THESEUS: What made you do that?

ADRASTOS: Apollo's riddles lured me.

THESEUS: What did Apollo advise for their marriages?   140

ADRASTOS: To give my girls to a boar and a lion.

THESEUS: How did you unravel that?

ADRASTOS: One night two exiles appeared at my door—

THESEUS: Who? Speak. There were two, you say?

ADRASTOS: Tydeus and Polynices. Fighting.

THESEUS: So you gave your daughters to those beasts?

ADRASTOS: Because they fought like animals.

THESEUS: Why had they left their fatherlands?

ADRASTOS: Tydeus spilled a kinsman's blood, and fled.

THESEUS: And Oedipus' son, why did he leave Thebes?   150

ADRASTOS: His father's curse, that he would kill his brother.

THESEUS: He was wise, then, to leave of his own free will.

ADRASTOS: Yes, but those at home robbed those who left.

THESEUS: His brother robbed him? In his absence?

ADRASTOS: I went to Thebes to right those wrongs. And lost.

THESEUS: Did you consult prophets and sacrificial fires?

ADRASTOS: That's just it, you've seen where I fell short.

THESEUS: So you went without the gods' favor, it seems.

ADRASTOS: Worse. I went against Amphiaraos' will.

THESEUS: You defied the gods so casually?   160

ADRASTOS: The younger men confused me with their uproar.

THESEUS: You were all courage, no second thought.

ADRASTOS: Yes. That has ruined many generals.
But, most stout-hearted leader in all Greece,
Lord of Athens, I fall in shame at your door,
touching your knee with my hand,
I, a gray-haired man, once a glorious king.
But now misfortune sets its heel on my neck.
Rescue our dead, take pity on my grief;
pity these mothers whose children have died.   170
Old and barren, they dared to travel here
to a foreign land, on legs too weak for walking.
They dared to come here, not
for Demeter's sacred mysteries, but to bury
their dead, those sons by whose hands
they should have received their own funeral rites.
Listen: it's as wise for a wealthy man to look on the poor,
as for the poor man to study the rich, and imitate,
to plant the love of money deep in his heart.
Fortunate men should pity the sorrow of others.   180
You'd be wise to learn from me, though my story's grim.
Take the poet: if he gives birth to a song
he joys in the birth. But if, like me, he grieves
from trouble at home, he can't please others:
that wouldn't be decent. You'll ask, no doubt
why we ignore Sparta and burden Athens
with such labor. It's only right that I answer.
Sparta is harsh, dishonest in her dealings;
Other cities are small and weak. Only yours
has the strength to take up such labor.   190
Athens takes notice of pain, and in you has
a noble, youthful shepherd: without such men
for generals, many cities have been destroyed.

CHORUS: Theseus, I join my plea
           to his: take up our cause.

THESEUS: I've wrestled with others in this argument:
           I've heard that life provides more pain than good.
           I beg to differ. Indeed, it seems to me
           that life abounds in goods for humankind.
           If it weren't the case we wouldn't still be here   200
           in the light of day. And I praise the god
           who brought our human life from savagery
           and delivered us from the condition of beasts.
           First he granted us reason, and then the tongue
           as messenger of words, to enable speech.
           He taught us to raise food, and down from heaven
           sent rain to nourish crops and quench our thirst.
           And that's not all: he taught us how to endure
           winter, and how to ward off the sun god's glare
           in summer, and gave us navigation so we can trade   210
           with neighbors whatever our own land lacks.
           As for mysteries and things we don't clearly know,
           our priests read them in fire and pry in the folds
           of entrails, and decipher birds in flight.
           Now, don't we seem pampered weaklings, demanding more
           when a god has given us such preparation for life?
           But we in our arrogance lust to know
           more than the god, and preening in pride of mind
           we think we're wiser than all the gods together.
           I'm afraid you're in that crowd, my friend, a fool   220
           binding your daughters up in prophecies
           and packing them off with strangers as if the gods
           had given them. You mixed the bright with the muddy,
           wounded your house. A wise man, now,
           never joins pure to impure bodies the way you've done:
           he brings only fine, prosperous friends into his house.
           For the god gives common fortunes to those who live
           in common, and destroys the blameless and healthy
           if they've touched infected ones.
                                         So, you led all the men
           of Argos into war, insulting your seers,   230

30

snubbing the gods; you wrecked your city.
You lost your wits to the youths, you say,
hoodlums roaring for glory no matter what
the cost, no matter how foolish the cause,
or how many citizens die, just so one boy
can play general, another grab hold of the state,
another get rich, with no regard at all
for the people, and how they will suffer.

                                     There are three
classes of citizens. The wealthy are useless, leeches
always sucking for more. As for the poor,   240
they're monsters, bums and beggars inflamed
with envy, itching to raid the rich,
at the mercy of party bosses. Of the three,
only the moderate class can save the city,
keep law and order, and guard the constitution.
And after your idiocy, you are expecting me
to be your ally? You think I can recommend
such plans to my people? Good day to you.
You've made your bed, now lie in it.

CHORUS: He made a mistake. It's common in the young.   250
          You ought to pardon this man here as well.
          We came in the hope, my lord, that you would heal us.

ADRASTOS: Theseus, I didn't come here looking for a judge.
          I don't need punishment and scolding
          for my errors. I came to ask your help.
          If you're not willing to give it, I accept
          your verdict, as I must. What else can I do?
          Come, old women, rouse yourselves. Leave your
          silvery suppliant branches on the ground
          and let the gods and Earth and Light of Sun   260
          and Demeter who carries fire be witnesses:
          we prayed to the gods, and nothing came of it.

CHORUS: Theseus, you're Aithra's son. She was born
          of Pittheus, son of Pelops. We of the land
          of Pelops share paternal blood with you.

What will you do? Will you betray your blood
and drive from your land old women who cannot obtain
what is rightfully theirs? Never! A beast has a cave
for shelter, a slave has altars, a city in storm
turns to another city. For nothing mortal remains   270
blessed straight through to the end.

The CHORUS *divides into two groups as they move from*
orchestra to stage and break into song.

A: Go, poor women, leave Persephone's
holy floor, go stretch your hands around his knees:
hold him, have him bring back those bodies tossed
beside the walls of Thebes where they were lost.

B: By your cheeks, I implore, oh noble king, our friend:
kneeling, I clutch your knee, your gracious hand.
Pity my lost sons, pity the surge
of my lament far from home, a mother's dirge.

A: Child, in your youth, don't scorn men the wolves will

                                       ravage 280
in Cadmus' land. They died: they were your age.

B: Look on my weeping: at your knees I crawl
and beg you—give my son a burial.

THESEUS: Mother, are you sobbing? Do you hide your face
in your delicate veil? Have these women's cries
affected you? They've pierced me as well.
Come, raise your white head. You mustn't weep
at Demeter's holy altar.

AITHRA: (*wails*)

THESEUS: You shouldn't suffer their grief.

AITHRA: Poor women, poor women.

THESEUS: You're not related to them.   290

AITHRA: My child, may I speak, for your own good, and for the city's?

THESEUS: Of course. Even women can talk good sense.

AITHRA: I'm afraid you'll disapprove what I have to say.

THESEUS: I'll disapprove if you hide good advice from us.

AITHRA: I'd rather speak, than later blame myself
for wrong-headed silence. Nor should fear
make me veil what I know to be right.

My son, first and foremost, it's the will of the gods
you have to consider, so you won't make some fatal mistake.
In this matter alone, my child, you've lost your way.   300
What's more, if we didn't have to be brave
for the sake of the innocent, I would hold my peace.
But you ought to know that this action will honor you,
and I enjoin you solemnly: you *must*
punish those violent men who keep
corpses from due burial and holy rites;
with your own hand you must strike
those bandits who confound the sacred laws
of all Greece. All civilized order rests
on this: the safekeeping of laws.
                                    And another thing: 310
you wouldn't want it said that you hung back,
afraid, when you could have wrested the crown
of fame for the city; that you battled a boar in sport
but faced with helmets and spearpoints, when you had
a real battle, man to man, you were found to be
a coward.
                    Never! My son, if you are indeed
my son, don't shame yourself. Do you not see
how your fatherland, rebuked for meddling,
stares back at accusers with wild Gorgon eyes?
In her labors she soars in strength and pride.   320

33

But peaceful cities, in shady diplomacy,
haggle behind the scenes for hidden ends.
So, child, won't you help the dead and their sorrowing
mothers, since they're in need? This is just cause
for war. And even though the Thebans have won
for now, I think they'll find a different throw
of the dice next time. The gods reverse everything.

CHORUS: Beloved Queen, you have spoken well to him,
and to me. We are twice rewarded.

THESEUS: The words I spoke, Mother, fit him perfectly   330
and I stand by my judgment
of those plans which ruined him. But I see
and accept the point of your correction.
I would not be Theseus if I fled
danger; with many heroic deeds
I have spread my reputation throughout all Greece:
Theseus, always the avenger of wrong.
So you are right. I cannot shun this labor.
What would my enemies say of me if you,
who gave me birth and who still fear for me,   340
are the first to bid me to take up such labor?
        I'll do it. I will go and free the dead
by words, if possible. If not, by spear.
The gods will not begrudge this. But I must have
the agreement of all Athens for such an act.
Athens will back me, since I wish it. But if I explain
I'll have the people more inclined to consent.
For I set them up as monarchs of themselves
and freed the city, giving them equal votes.
Taking Adrastos, then, to confirm my words,   350
I'll go to the citizens. When they're persuaded
I'll rouse the best youths of Athens and return
here. Prepared for battle, I'll send word
to Creon, demanding the bodies of the dead.
        But, old women, set my mother free
from your garlands so I can lead her home
by her dear hand. A child who will not serve

34

his parents degrades his life. Such service is
our noblest gift. A man's care for his parents
is given him by his children in their turn.   360

Exeunt THESEUS, AITHRA, ADRASTOS. (*the sons of the
Dead move off the stage into the orchestra, where they
will sit in silence until the end of the fourth episode,*
[954])

CHORUS:

STR Argos rippling with horses, my father's field,
hear the king speak, hear
matters sacred to the gods,
glory for Argos and the Peloponnese.

ANT Let him press till all my sorrow is repealed,
let him carry here
my prize soiled in blood,
let his help to the land of Argos bind him to us.

STR This holy labor brings an honored prize
to our cities, and gratitude   370
forever. What will Athens do?
Befriend us? Bury the sons we bore?

ANT Protect her, protect the mother, city of Pallas.
Take care: don't stain the laws
of mortals. You honor justice, it's true,
cut back the wicked, rescue the injured and poor.

THESEUS *returns, from right, with* ADRASTOS *and an
Athenian herald onto the stage.*

THESEUS: Herald, you know your trade, serving
the city, and me, with your proclamations. Now,
cross the rivers to Thebes and report
to their proud ruler: 380
"Theseus bids you, as a favor, bury the dead.
He speaks as your neighbor, worthy of courtesy,

and wants to insure Athenian friendship with all."
If the Thebans agree, praise them and march
straight home. If not, make this other speech:
"Attend our party, and our sharpened spears."
The army is camped and ready for war, nearby,
in ranks by Demeter's holy spring.
And the Athenians were more than pleased to accept this labor
since they knew I wished it.

                          Who is this   390
interrupting us? I'd say a Theban herald
by his dress. See what he wants. He may relieve
you of your labor: his visit is well timed.

       Enter Theban HERALD, *from left, onto the stage.*

HERALD: Who is the sovereign here? To whom should I report
          Creon's words? He rules now in Thebes
          since Eteokles died at the seven-mouthed gates
          killed by his brother, Polynices.

THESEUS: You've already begun badly, stranger,
          when you seek one master here. Our city is free,
          not run by a single man. The people rule   400
          by turns in yearly succession. So our poor
          have equal voting power with the rich.

HERALD: You've given me the advantage in this game.
          Our city is ruled by one man, not a mob.
          No one there buffets the city this way and that
          with windy boasts, all for private profit,
          quick with the soft touch and backroom favors,
          then milking the city dry, concealing old graft
          with new, ducking all prosecution. And, besides,
          if the people can't distinguish true from false,   410
          how can they keep the city safe on course?
          Knowledge comes with experience, not in a flash.
          Even if a peasant were not an ignorant clod,
          with all his labors, he would not have time
          to look to the common good. Indeed,

for the upper class, it's a disease, when, fresh
from his ditch, some dirt farmer bridles the mob
and drives it with the witchery of his tongue.

THESEUS: Well, what a clever herald! Moonlighting
      as an orator. Since you started this argument,   420
      now listen. You began the debate.
      There is nothing worse for a city than a sovereign,
      when first no laws are common, and he rules
      alone, taking himself for law. That way
      nothing is equal. But when the laws are written,
      the poor man and the rich have equal rights.
      Then, when a wealthy citizen does wrong,
      a weaker one can criticize, and prevail,
      with justice on his side. *That's* liberty.
      Anyone with sound advice for the city's good   430
      can make it public and shine among his peers.
      The reticent keep quiet. What could be
      more equal or beneficial for the city?
      What's more, when the people rule their land
      they delight in the young men growing up.
      But a single lord finds that intolerable
      and those whom he judges noble or smart
      he kills, to preserve his reign. How then
      can a city thrive, when someone hacks the spears
      of wheat from the spring field, and harvests our young?   440
      Why should we gather a living for our children
      if it's just a tyrant's livelihood we swell?
      Why keep our daughters virtuously at home,
      sweetmeats for the tyrant's passing urge,
      tears for their parents? Let him die
      if he marries my child by force.

                              Now, all these points
      I pit against yours. What do you want from our land?
      If this weren't official business, you'd return
      in tears, for all your cant. A messenger
      should state his errand and leave in double time.   450
      Next time Creon sends a man to Athens
      let it be someone more tight-lipped than you.

CHORUS: Whenever a god lets the corrupt prosper
they gorge on pride, thinking their luck will last.

HERALD: A word, if you permit? On these sore points
let's agree to disagree. Creon proclaims:
"I and the people of Thebes refuse
Adrastos entry into Athenian land.
If he is there, drive him out, I say
before the god's light sinks; scatter the suppliants'   460
sacred boughs. Do not take up
his dead by force: you have no business with Argos.
If you obey me, you'll steer your city safe
across calm water. But if you refuse
a wave of spears will crash upon us all."
Consider well, and since you claim your city's free,
don't let my message goad you to reply
in rash rage when you stand on weaker ground.
Don't trust in hope: it's sent many cities to war
whipping them into frenzy. Whenever war   470
comes up for the people's vote, no one counts on
his own death; each thinks the other man
will suffer. But if death rose before your eyes
when you cast your vote, Greece in its craze for spears
would not be destroyed in battle. All men know
which of two words is better: between peace and war,
which is evil and which good, and how much more
peace benefits humankind. She is most dear
to the Muses, hated by Vengeance. She loves
strong children, she rejoices in wealth. But we   480
choose war, in our evil, and enslave the weak,
man lording it over man, town over town.
        But will you still help those despised dead, burying
those killed by criminal pride? Surely Capaneus'
thundered body should still smoke—
he who hurled the very ladders at the gates,
swearing to smash the city, whatever god willed?
And didn't a whirlwind snatch the fortune-teller,
flinging his four-horse chariot into a chasm?
Don't the other captains lie at the gates of Thebes,   490

skulls shattered by rocks? Either you boast
you now know better than Zeus, or you'll confess
the gods were right to kill those hell-bent men.

To sum it up: A wise man loves, first, his children,
then parents and country, which he should protect,
not ruin. A hothead leader, a young captain,
spells danger. A man calm in crisis is wise.
In fact, courage truly defined is: foresight.

CHORUS: Zeus punished them enough. There was no need
for you to be so proud, beating down their pride.   500

ADRASTOS: You vicious—

THESEUS: Silence, Adrastos. Hold your tongue.
Don't thrust in your speeches before mine.
He came heralding to me, not you, this fellow,
and I must answer him.

THESEUS *turns to the* HERALD.

Now, point by point
I'll answer you. First, I am not aware
That Creon has the right to order me,
or is the stronger, so Athens must obey.
The world would be upside down if we let ourselves
be bullied so. And another point: I didn't start the war,
I didn't march with them onto Theban soil.   510
But burying the corpses, I bring no harm
to Thebes, I threaten no war. I'm in the right
preserving the holy law of all the Greeks.
What's wrong in this?
                    Granted the Argives hurt you,
they are dead. You beat back the enemy
honorably, and shamed them. Justice was done.
Now, let the corpses be hidden in the earth
from which each came to light; let soul release
to air, body to earth. We do not own
our bodies, but are mere tenants there for life,   520

and earth that nursed them takes them back again.
Do you think you punish Argos, not burying the dead?
Far from it. This is the common creed of Greece
to ensure that no one keeps the dead from burial
and proper rites. Brave men would turn cowardly
if your deeds became the law.

      So you came threatening me
with frightful words, yet you fear the dead
if they're buried? Why? Can they destroy your land
when buried? Can children in earth's womb
beget revenge? This is nonsense, to fear   530
such phantoms.

     You fools, think of life's
real struggle. Some mortals thrive
now, some will in the future, others did in the past.
The god prospers, anyway. A man in trouble
placates the god in hope of better days;
a rich man, fearing for his life, reveres
the god as well. Knowing these struggles,
you shouldn't rage at such small injury,
or harm your city with injustices.

  What do we ask? Give back the dead   540
and let us bury them with reverence.
Or else it's clear: I'll bury them
by force. It will never be said in Greece
that the gods' ancient law, coming to me
and to Athens was despised.

CHORUS: Take heart. Most men will praise
you if you save the light of justice.

HERALD: Shall I oblige you with a brief reply?

THESEUS: Speak, if you wish. You're not the silent type.

HERALD: You'll never take the Argive children from our land. 550

THESEUS: Now listen, if you'll be so kind.

HERALD: Of course. I wouldn't keep you from your turn.

THESEUS: I shall carry the dead from Thebes, and bury them.

HERALD: You'll have to test the case with shields.

THESEUS: I've survived many other labors.

HERALD: Your father raised you to conquer everything?

THESEUS: Only the proud. We do not punish the good.

HERALD: You're truly enterprising, you and your city.

THESEUS: Yes. Athens' great labor wins great reward.

HERALD: Come! Our dragon spears will hurl you in the dust.   560

THESEUS: What god of war is born from a dragon's tooth?

HERALD: Suffering will teach you that. You're still a whelp.

THESEUS: You won't enrage me with your boasts. Get out,
leave our land, pack up your empty words.
It's pointless, talking.

                              Exit HERALD, *to the left.*

                    Now, we must marshall
every foot soldier and charioteer,
and horseman, foam flecking the bit, to charge
to Thebes. I'll march to their seven gates,
myself the captain with iron in my hand,
myself the herald. As for you, Adrastos,   570
wait. Don't mix your fortunes with mine.
With my own guardian spirit I'll command
the army, a fresh man with a fresh spear.
I need only one thing: the support of all those gods
who honor justice. If I can count on them,

41

victory is mine. A man can never win
glory without a god at his side.

Exit to the left all actors except ADRASTOS, *who remains*
onstage.

CHORUS: (*in two groups*)

STR A: Useless mothers of useless generals—
        What green terror lodges in my entrails?

                        Enter MESSENGER, *from the left, onto stage.*

B: What news do you bring? What word is this?   580

A: How will Athena's army stand the test?

B: Did you speak with spears, or word to word?

A: May victory come! But if Ares preferred
    death, if the city fills with groans,
    with gashes, blood, and beaten breasts,
    what word, what accusation, will be heard?

ANT B: Thebes' luck may turn this time, and quench her fire:
        this hope binds courage all around my fear.

A: You speak of the spirits of justice.

B: What others give fortune to us?   590

A: The gods give many things for man to bear.

B: You are undone by an old fear.
    Justice called to justice, death to death.
    The gods, who know how everything on earth
    will end, grant ease to mortal care.

STR A: How can we leave the Demeter's flashing stream
and reach the mighty towers of the plain?

B: If some god winged your feet, you'd fly
to Thebes' two rivers: you would see
your friends, and you would know their fate first hand.   600

A: What lot, what fortune crouches for the brave king of this land?

ANT B: We call on gods we have called before:
they are our first defense against fear.

A: Zeus, who begot the heifer, ancient mother of Inachos,
be a faithful ally to Athens, protecting us.

B: Bring the prize, the city's guardians, in their shame:
Carry them here to the funeral flame.

MESSENGER: Women, I come with happy news, both my own escape
and Theseus' victory. I was captured
in that war the seven captains waged   610
against Thebes, by the River Dirce.
But I'll spare you a long account.
I served Capaneus, whom Zeus killed,
thundered to cinders with his lightning bolt.

CHORUS: What joy, to hear of your return,
and Theseus' success. But if the whole army
of Athens is safe, that will be blessed news.

MESSENGER: Safe. And it achieved what Adrastos ought
to have done, with the Argives, when he marched from home
by the River Inachos to take Thebes.

CHORUS: How did Theseus,   620
grandson of Aigeus, and his troops claim victory?
Speak! You were there: tell us: we were far away.

43

MESSENGER: A dazzling blade of sunlight, a clear rod,
struck the earth. There, on a tower, I stood
at Elektra's gate, I could watch everything.
I saw Athenians, three divisions, come:
on the right flank, infantry stretched
up the hill of Ismene, as they call it there;
Theseus, famous heir of Aigeus, led:
his men were of old Athenian blood.   630
On the left came Paralos holding high his spear
as far as the spring of Ares. Flanking the foot soldiers
rode the cavalry in detachments
of equal number. Chariots massed below
Amphion's sacred tomb. The Theban troops
waited by the walls, keeping the dead
behind them—the dead for whom all fought. Horsemen stood
poised against horsemen, chariots against chariots.
Then Theseus' herald made this speech:
"Silence, troops. Silence there, in the Theban ranks.   640
Listen. We come to retrieve the dead
and bury them. We wish to protect the law
of all the Greeks, not to threaten death."
Creon said nothing, but stood among his men
without a word. Then chariots launched the war,
hurtling through each other's ranks to place
their fighters in formation. Swordsmen clashed,
the chariots drove back into the melee
charging the infantry. When the captains saw
the turmoil, they joined the fight: Phorbas, leader   650
of the Athenian cavalry, and the Theban marshalls
surged and staggered back in waves.
I saw it all, I didn't just hear of it—
I stood where the chariots and the horsemen fought.
How can I tell it? I saw such agonies:
dust storming up to heaven, choking-thick;
men flailing up and down, yanked by reins;
rivers of blood from foot soldiers, and riders
catapulted from chariots, pitched headlong
to the ground alongside splintered cars.   660
When he saw our horsemen conquering, Creon snatched

44

a shield, and stalked into the battle swarm to keep
his allies from despair. Theseus' men
would have been routed then and there, but the young king
seized shining arms, and plunged into the fight.
Core against core, the armies slammed together;
they butchered and were butchered, and with great cries
roared out commands to one another:
"Smash Thebes!" "Slash Athens with your spear!"
That army of men born from dragon's teeth   670
was a deadly force: it splintered our left flank.
But their right wing collapsed. The fight was even.
And this is where Theseus truly must be praised.
He didn't just ride on the crest of his success,
but rushed to the spot where his men were faltering.
He let out his battle cry, and shook the earth:
"Boys, if you don't beat back those Dragon Men,
we're lost!" He rallied courage throughout his ranks;
he himself snatched up the Epidaurian mace,
that terrifying club, and whirled it round: 680
he mowed down heads and helmets, snapping off
neck stalks with his wood. They could hardly stumble
over their feet fast enough to flee.
I howled for joy and danced deliriously,
clapping my hands. They poured up to the gates.
Throughout the city rose wails from young and old:
in terror, they jammed the temples. The Athenians could
have roared in through the gates, but Theseus
checked his men. "We didn't come to destroy
the city, " he cried," but to rescue the dead."   690
That's the kind of general to choose, one brave
against all odds, who hates the arrogant mob—
that mob which, though prosperous, tries to climb
the ladder's highest rung, and wrecks that fortune
that required better care.

CHORUS: Unhoped-for day! I see it, true at last,
          and now I believe in the gods. The horror subsides
          since Thebes has been brought to justice.

ADRASTOS: Zeus, why do we mortals
boast of intellect? We depend on you,   700
we obey your slightest wish. Argos was not,
as we thought, invincible, though we were young,
strong of arm, and many. When Eteokles
offered to compromise on moderate terms,
we refused, and were destroyed. But the Thebans then,
reveling in good luck like an upstart beggar
newly come into money, swelled with pride
and in that pride they, also, were destroyed.
Foolish mortals: you don't obey your friends
but circumstance. And cities, which could resolve   710
their differences through words, conclude affairs
with butchery instead. But enough of this:
I want to hear your escape, and then the rest.

MESSENGER: While the confusion of battle rocked the city,
I slipped through the gates where the Thebans came
                                        streaming in.

ADRASTOS: And did you bring the dead they were fighting for?

MESSENGER: No. Only the seven famous captains.

ADRASTOS: What happened to the common soldiers who died?

MESSENGER: They were buried by Cithaeron's folds.

ADRASTOS: On which side of the mountain? Who buried them?   720

MESSENGER: Theseus did, on this side, by Eleutherae's shady ridge.

ADRASTOS: Where have you left the dead he did not bury?

MESSENGER: Nearby. A short distance, for swift desire.

ADRASTOS: Did it trouble the servants to carry them from the field?

MESSENGER: No slave took part in that labor.

ADRASTOS: Theseus carried the corpses?

MESSENGER: So you'd say, if you'd seen how he cared for the dead.

ADRASTOS: He himself washed the poor men's wounds?

MESSENGER: Exactly. He laid out the beds, and covered their limbs.

ADRASTOS: What a terrible burden and shame to take on himself!   730

MESSENGER: Why should we think of our common griefs as shame?

ADRASTOS: Oh gods—I wish I had died with them.

MESSENGER: Your laments are useless. You're making the women weep.

ADRASTOS: Yes. They are my teachers now.
But I'll go raise my hands to greet the dead
and pour out the hymns of Death for my friends
who have left me in my misery to weep
alone. This is the only mortal loss
whose expense can't be recovered: the mortal soul.
Lost money can be restored, not human life.   740

Exeunt MESSENGER *and* ADRASTOS *to the left.*

CHORUS:
STR My joy is woven with sorrow.
Glory crowns the city
and double glory crowns
the generals and their spears.
But for me to look on my son's
corpse, is horror and beauty—
longed-for, unhoped-for day,
seen at last, greatest in tears.

ANT Time, the ancient father
of days, should have let me stay   750
unmarried forever here.

47

Why did I need sons?
I shouldn't have had to bear
this pain if I'd been free
of marriage, but now I see
the worst: loved children torn from my arms.

Enter, from the left, ADRASTOS *and ten Athenian pall
bearers, who carry the Argive corpses to the stage.*

CHORUS: (*chant*)
But here are the bodies now
of my lost children. How
can I die with my children,
going down to Hades in common?   760

STR (*lyric exchange between* ADRASTOS *and* CHORUS)

ADRASTOS: Shout, oh mothers, cry
for the dead going under the ground:
wail responses to my
groans for their burial mound.

CHORUS: Children, bitter target
of your loving mother's moan:
I call to you, though you are dead.

ADRASTOS: Ai ai—

CHORUS: Of all my sorrows, I . . .

ADRASTOS: Ai ai—

CHORUS: —Ai ai

ADRASTOS: We have suffered—

CHORUS: —obscene grief.   770

ADRASTOS: City of Argos, do you see what has happened to me?

CHORUS: And you see me ripped from my sons.

ADRASTOS:

ANT Bring in the bodies, soaked in blood,
            of those unlucky dead,
        Shamefully slain by the shameful
            on whose battleground they fell.

CHORUS: Give him here, let me hold my boy
            folded in my embrace,
            let my hands caress his face.

ADRASTOS: You hold, you hold—

CHORUS: —the weight of the world.   780

ADRASTOS: Ai ai—

CHORUS: Why don't you speak to the parents?

ADRASTOS: Hear me.

CHORUS: You groan for both of us.

ADRASTOS: I wish the Thebans had struck me down in the dust.

CHORUS: I wish my body had never been yoked
            to a husband's bed.

ADRASTOS:

EPODE A gulf stretches before you, mothers
            torn from your sons.

CHORUS: I've raked my face with my fingernails, I've poured
            ashes on my head.

            Enter THESEUS, *with some young Athenian soldiers,*
                                onto the stage.

ADRASTOS: (*wails*) Let earth gape and swallow me, let a storm   790
    rip through me, let the flame
    of Zeus crash my skull.

CHORUS: You see those bitter marriages
      and Apollo's bitter tale.
    The Fury, slinking from Oedipus' house,
      drags his groans to us.

THESEUS: I wanted to ask, but couldn't interrupt
    the lament you poured out for the army. Since I let it pass,
    let me question you now, Adrastos.
    How did these men attain such heights of courage   800
    among mortals? Since you are wiser, speak
    to the young men of the city. You know the facts.
    All they know is that the heroes' deeds,
    besieging the city, were greater than words can tell.
    But I won't make a joke of it by demanding
    a blow by blow account, who stood against whom
    in battle, and the spear wounds each received.
    That's idle chatter, for listener and teller both,
    and nonsense to think a man plunged in fighting
    with a hail of spears before his eyes, could see   810
    clearly enough to tell who's been heroic.
    I couldn't bring myself to ask such things,
    or believe them, if someone tried to trot them out.
    A man meeting the enemy head on
    can hardly see what he really has to see.

ADRASTOS: Hear me, then. I am happy to take up
    this charge of yours, eager to praise
    my friends with truth and justice.
    Do you see that man, shattered by the lightning bolt?
    That is Capaneus. He had massive wealth   820
    but took no pride in it. He set his sights
    no higher than a poor man, fleeing those
    who heap their tables up with luxuries
    and spurn what will suffice. He took delight
    not in stuffing his stomach, but in moderation.

He was a true friend to friends, both near and far:
there are not many like that: honest to a fault,
courteous, and as dutiful at home
as to his fellow citizens.

               The second
I praise is Eteoklos. His honesty   830
was of a different kind. A poor youth,
he later rose to eminence in Argos.
And though friends often offered him gold, he shied
from it, and would not bind himself
by taking slavish gifts. He loathed
guilty persons, not the whole city of Thebes,
since a city should not be blamed
if its captain steers it wrong.

                  The third I praise
is Hippomedon. As a child, he dared
already to spurn the arts and the cushioned life,   840
but roamed the fields, with a taste for the roughest tasks.
He delighted in feats of courage, loved the hunt
and horses and the bow taut in his hand.
He trained his body as a useful gift to Argos.

    And I praise the child of the huntress Atalanta,
Parthenopaios, that handsome boy.
He was Arcadian, but came to our River
Inachos, and was trained in Argos.
There he reached manhood. He took great care—
as is right for a resident alien in the town—   850
not to make trouble or envy the city's wealth
or stir up quarrels, which weigh upon us,
whether from citizen or foreigner.
He joined the army just like a native Argive,
defended the land, cheered at the city's success,
and grieved if the city were harmed

    Great praise of Tydeus may be brief.
Not in speeches, he shone, but in his shield;
terribly expert, butcher of the untrained.
In mind his brother Meleager far outstripped him,   860
but Tydeus won equal fame in the art of the spear,
and drew his own music from his ringing shield.

Do not be amazed, Theseus, hearing all this,
that these men dared to die at the towers of Thebes.
Noble upbringing begets nobility.
Any man trained in virtue is ashamed
to do a wrong. And this high courage
can be taught, just as a babe is taught
to speak and listen to things he doesn't know.
Lessons learned early stay with us till old age.   870
So train your children well.

CHORUS: (*breaking into song*)
Child, it was for doom
    I carried you in my womb:
    and labored in Herculean pain.
Now Death takes as his spoil
    the fruit of my laboring toil:
    I am aged, untended, alone
    though I begot a son.

THESEUS: We must also praise Amphiaraos, the noble child
of Oikles. The gods clearly singled him out   880
for honor by dragging him and his horses, still alive,
into the folds of the earth. And Oedipus' son,
Polynices, we can truthfully praise.
He was my guest when he first fled from Thebes,
before, by his own choice, he went on to Argos.
But do you know what I plan to do with these men?

ADRASTOS: I know only one thing: to obey your every word.

THESEUS: Capaneus, struck by Zeus' fire—

ADRASTOS: —You'll bury him apart, as a holy corpse?

THESEUS: Yes. But the others will all go in a single pyre.   890

ADRASTOS: Where will you set Capaneus' tomb?

THESEUS: By the temple: I'll build it in stone.

ADRASTOS: The slaves should see to that labor.

THESEUS: No, we'll take care of these.

(*to attendants*) Carry off the dead.

ADRASTOS: Go, bereaved mothers, approach your children.

The CHORUS *move toward the biers at the edge of the
stage.*

THESEUS: That is the worst thing you could advise, Adrastos.

ADRASTOS: What do you mean? Shouldn't mothers touch their children?

THESEUS: They would die, seeing the mutilation.

ADRASTOS: It's a bitter sight, the blood and wounds of the dead.

THESEUS: Then why do you want to inflict such pain?   900

ADRASTOS: I give in. (*to* CHORUS) Be brave, and stay there.

The CHORUS *abruptly come to a halt; they never reached
the stage.*

Theseus is right. When they've burned on the pyre,
you can embrace their bones.

*Attendants begin to carry Argive corpses behind the
skēnē.*

Tormented race of man,
why do you take up spears, and bring down death
upon each other? Stop! Leave off those labors,
guard your city in peace. The needs of life
are small. You should provide for them
gently, without such gruesome labor.

53

Exeunt THESEUS *and* ADRASTOS *behind the skēnē; the stage is now empty. The secondary chorus of the sons of the Dead leave their position in the orchestra, move across the stage and exeunt behind the skēnē. The theater is now empty except for the* CHORUS *of mothers.*

CHORUS:

STR   No longer blessed with child, not blessed   910
      with son, I am cursed
      among full-wombed Argive women.
And Artemis, goddess of birth,
      won't visit those who are barren.
Life without life, I roam,
      a cloud darting high over earth,
      in winter's storm.

ANT   Seven mothers, we brought to the world
      seven sons whom Argos called
      glorious: but we endure in pain.   920
Now, without son, without child,
      I grow old, grieving alone;
neither dead nor alive, but set
      apart from all, compelled
      by my estranging fate.

EPODE   Tears only remain
and useless mementos of my son
in empty rooms, and my own cropped hair
without a wreath, and libations poured
over the dead, and songs which the golden Lord   930
Apollo will not accept. I'll rise
each morning weeping, and drench my eyes
and every fold of my gown
on my breast with tears for my son.

And now I see Capaneus' funeral chamber,
      his sacred tomb, and just outside
      the temple door, Theseus' funeral gifts
      for the rescued dead.

EVADNE *appears on a cliff overhanging Demeter's*
temple.

Look! here comes Evadne, the peerless wife
of Capaneus, struck by Zeus' bolt,   940
Evadne, daughter of Iphis. Why is she climbing
the path? Why does she take her stand
high on the airy rock
which towers over the shrine?

EVADNE: (*solo aria*)
STR   What torchlight, what brilliant glare
did sun and moon drive through the air
       with nymphs swiftly banishing shade
when the city of Argos, proud,
       towering, ringing with song
       exulted the whole day long   950
       at my marriage to glorious
       bronze-armored Capaneus?
I've rushed here from my house
like a Maenad running loose
to see the pyre's light and the holy tomb,
       and to lead my soul
       from life's long toil
into Death's great room.
Death is voluptuous,
       to die with our lovers   960
       if the god lets it come to pass.

CHORUS: And you can see, from where you stand, just under you,
the pyre, Zeus' treasure-chest, where
your husband lies, mastered by the brilliant bolt.

EVADNE:
ANT   Yes, I see my deliverance.
Fate keeps step with my dance.
       For glory I'll cast myself

from this jut of cliff
    and leap to the funeral pyre:
melting in radiant flame   970
      my body will mingle with yours,
      loved husband, flesh to flesh,
      down in Persephone's house—
      I'll never betray your death
by clinging to life on earth.
      Sunlight, goodbye. Goodbye,
marriage. Not for me those
beds of virtuous
      weddings which bring
forth children to Argos.   980
My true wedded husband
    melts in a pure wind
    with his wife in a single fire.

CHORUS: Look: here comes Iphis himself, your father:
he will grieve at your strange words.

            Enter IPHIS, *from the left, onto the stage.*

IPHIS: Women of sorrow, I come, a most sorrowful
old man, with a double grief. I must bring home
by ship Eteoklos, my son, killed
by a Theban spear. And I must find my daughter,
Capaneus' wife, who fled from home in frenzy   990
and yearns to die with him. Till now, I've kept
her guarded in the house. But in this new
turmoil, I released the guards, and now
she's fled. But she must have come here.
Have you seen her?

EVADNE: Why ask those women?
Here I am on the rock, perched like a bird
over Capaneus' pyre, hovering
in sorrow, Father.

IPHIS: Child, what wind, what voyage, what reason 1000
made you steal away from home and find this land?

56

EVADNE: My plans would anger you if you heard them,
so I can't tell you, Father.

IPHIS: What? It's not right for your father to know?

EVADNE: You wouldn't know how to judge what I have in mind.

IPHIS: Why have you dressed yourself up so gorgeously?

EVADNE: A special glory requires it, Father.

IPHIS: You don't look like a wife in mourning.

EVADNE: I have dressed myself for quite another purpose.

IPHIS: Then why come here, to the tomb and the pyre?   1010

EVADNE: Because here I'll win glory in victory.

IPHIS: What victory? What are you talking about?

EVADNE: Victory over all women under the sun.

IPHIS: By handicrafts, or by some work of the mind?

EVADNE: By heroic action. I shall lie with my husband in death.

IPHIS: What are you saying? What is this rotten riddle?

EVADNE: I shall leap right here into Capaneus' pyre.

IPHIS: Daughter—you haven't told this to anyone?

EVADNE: On the contrary: I want all Argos to know.

IPHIS: I'll never permit such a thing.   1020

EVADNE: It's useless. You can't reach me, can't take my hand.
My body falls: whatever you suffer
my husband and I burn together.

57

EVADNE *leaps into flames, behind skēnē.* CHORUS *and*
IPHIS *break into song.*

CHORUS: Woman, what horror!

IPHIS: I am finished, daughters of Argos.

CHORUS: To have lived through such savagery—
            can you bear to see what she dared?

IPHIS: You couldn't find a more broken man on earth.

CHORUS: Poor wounded man:
            Oedipus' fate has touched you,   1030
            you, and my whole city.

IPHIS: Oh gods, why can't mortals have a second youth
       and then grow old again? In daily life
       at home, if something fails, we patch it up
       and make it better second time around.
       But a whole life-course never comes again.
       If we were young and old twice over
       we could correct all mistakes on the second try.
       I used to envy others who had children
       and thought I would die with desire for my own.   1040
       But if I had known the suffering that comes
       from losing children, I wouldn't be here now
       in this nightmare, having a noble son
       born to me, then suddenly snatched away.
           So be it. Now what can I do?
       Go home? And see that echoing void
       in room after room, my whole life out of place?
       Or should I stay by Capaneus' tomb?
       Life was sweetest then, when I had my girl.
       But she is gone, who used to kiss my cheeks   1050
       and hold my head in her hands. For an aging father,
       nothing is gentler than a girl.
       Sons are nobler of soul, but daughters give
       softest caresses.

Won't you lead me away, quickly,
lead me away and shut me in the dark,
and let my old body melt away without food
and die? What good would it do me
to touch my daughter's bones?
  Old age, I despise this wrestle with you.
I despise those fools who coax out life's last days   1060
with fancy diets and potions and witchery,
diverting life's course, trying to bypass death.
They ought, rather, when they're useless with old age,
to clear out of the way and leave room for the young.

Exit IPHIS, *to the left; from behind the skēnē enter sons of
the Dead and servants, who carry the ashes and bones of
the Dead in jars onto the stage.*

CHORUS: (*turning to personal attendants and chanting*)
The bones—they're bearing the bones
    of my dead children. No,
    hold me, I can't stand alone—
    I'm too weak from sorrow—
I've dragged out too long a life,
    melting in grief after grief: 1070
    what greater grief can there be
    for mortals, than to see
    our own children, ash and bone.

*The sons of the Dead advance and receive the funerary
jars. Lyric exchange between sons and mothers of the
                                                    Dead.*

CHILDREN:
  STR I bear them, I bear them—
      Sad mother, I bear my father's bones from the flame.
      So heavy they are, so weighted with grief, my whole
          life in a jar so small.

CHORUS: (*wails*)
      Child, bring your beloved
          mother these tears for the dead,

this small heap of ash, not the great   1080
        bodies that once paced Mycenae's street.

CHILDREN:

    ANT You are childless, childless,
         and I am torn from my father in distress,
         in lonely hallways, orphaned,
             wrenched from my father's hand.

    CHORUS: (*wails*)
         Where are the pangs of labor? the nights beguiled
             by long watches over the sleeping child?
         Where are the suckling, the rocking, the tenderness
             of kissing his sweet face?

CHILDREN:

    STR They are gone. Forever. My father—   1090
         They are gone—

    CHORUS: —into air.
         Their bodies have melted into ash and fire,
             to the Underworld they have flown.

CHILDREN: Father, do you hear your children mourn?
         Will I ever avenge your death with my own shield?
         May that day come for your child.

    ANT With god willing, we may win
         justice for our fathers.

         Movement of CHORUS *and sons toward each other stops.*

    CHORUS: Enough pain!
         Enough sorrow, enough   1100
             fruitless grief.

CHILDREN: One day the River Asopus at Thebes will shine
         and receive me as I march, leading the men of Argos
         in bronze armor to avenge my father's loss.

STR Father, you seem to hover before my eyes—

CHORUS: Leaning close to clasp and kiss—

CHILDREN: But your heartening message flies
        into thin air and disappears.

CHORUS: He left a double grief: one for the mother,
one for the son who will grieve forever.   1110

CHILDREN:
   ANT The burden crushes out my life.

CHORUS: Let me smear my breast with ash.

CHILDREN: I hate these words of grief:
        My heart extinguishes.

CHORUS: Child, you are gone. My prize, my joy:
I'll never rock you to sleep, my lovely boy.

Enter THESEUS *and* ADRASTOS *onto the stage.*

THESEUS: Adrastos and women of Argos, look on these
children. They hold their noble fathers' bodies
in both hands, bodies which I won.
The City of Athens and I entrust them to these boys.   1120
But we count on you to commemorate our kindness,
to preserve the memory of those whom we restored,
by recounting it to the children, and passing it on
from father to son, into posterity.
Thus you will remember always to honor Athens.
May Zeus and the gods in heaven witness what
a debt to us you take away with you.

ADRASTOS: Theseus, we witness all those noble deeds
you performed for the Land of Argos, in our need.
You have our undying thanks. I am forever   1130
in debt to the grandeur of your help to us.

61

THESEUS: What further service may I render you?

ADRASTOS: Fare well, and prosper. You and your city deserve it.

THESEUS: We shall indeed fare well. May you also thrive.

Enter ATHENA, *in full armor with helmet, aegis, and*
spear, on a concealed platform on the roof of the skēnē.

ATHENA: Listen, Theseus, to Athena's words.
I tell you what you must do to ensure this pact.
Do not give up the bones so easily,
letting the Argive children carry them off.
In return for the pains you and your city have taken
an oath must be sworn. Adrastos, here, must swear it.   1140
He is king, and can make a treaty for all Argos.
The treaty shall be: "Argos will never come
as a hostile force invading Athenian soil.
And if others invade, Argos will fend them off."
If they violate the oath, and attack Athens,
pray that the Land of Argos be destroyed.
Now listen to the method of the sacrifice.
You have a bronze-footed tripod in the house;
Heracles left it when he had just sacked Troy
and was rushing off to perform some other feat: 1150
he pledged you to set it up at the shrine at Delphi.
Cut the throats of three lambs in it, and inscribe the oaths
in the tripod's hollow basin. Then offer it
to Apollo at his shrine in Delphi, to preserve
as a memorial of the oaths, and a witness to Greece.
As for the biting knife with which you slit
the lambs' throats, bury it in the earth
there by the seven heroes' pyres. If Argos
ever marches on Athens, the knife, revealed,
will strike them with terror and bring them evil luck.   1160
Accomplish these rites, and then release the bones.
Then build a shrine where the sacred pyres burned
at the triple crossroads by the road to Argos.
This I declare. But to the Argive children

62

I proclaim: reach manhood, and destroy Thebes.
Avenge your fathers' deaths. You, Aigialeus,
instead of your father Adrastos, will lead the assault,
along with Tydeus' son, Diomedes.
Hold back for now: wait till your beards have grown
to rush as the bronze army of Argos against   1170
the seven-mouthed gates of Thebes.
You will be bitter for them: you have been nursed
as lion cubs, destroyers, doom of Thebes.
It shall be so. Epigoni, you will be called,
Avenging Sons. Your fame will resound in song,
so mighty an army you'll form, as you march with the god.

THESEUS: Queen Athena, I shall obey your words.
You straighten my path, you keep me from all error.
I shall bind this man to an oath. For only you
guide me in justice. If you look kindly on us   1180
we will flourish safely for all time to come.

CHORUS: Come, Adrastos, let us swear a vow
to Theseus and his city. It is just
to honor those who have given us their best.

NOTES ON THE TEXT

ORCHESTRA AND STAGE

Greek (really Athenian) tragedy is organized by alternating rhythms of speaking roles (episodes) and choral song/dance (*odes*). Formal distinctions in dialect, meter, and movement set these two voices of the drama clearly apart. The Theater of Dionysus, with its twin spaces of orchestra and stage, may well have helped to accent those formal structures of tragedy which distinquish choral from actors' parts. While our knowledge of the fifth-century theater is unfortunately meager, most scholars believe that by 420 B.C. the Theater of Dionysus consisted of a circular orchestra joined to a slightly raised, narrow rectangular stage (called the *logeion*) behind. Stairs, of no more than three or four steps, made communication between the two spaces possible.

Behind the stage, there was a building called a *skēnē*. As well as appearing in the orchestra and stage, actors could also appear above this building, either by being suspended from a crane known now as *deus ex machina* or by standing on a platform, called a *theologoeion* (the place for divine address), near the roof of the *skēnē* hidden from the audience's view, though in point of fact neither the *machina* or the *theologeion* was used exclusively for divine personages. The theater thus offered a tripartite order (orchestra, stage, and area above the *skēnē*) which, like the Globe Theater of Shakespearean London, suggested the structure of the *kosmos*. That is, in the shape of the theater we witness the interaction between the chorus, who in some fashion represent our common humanity, in the orchestra; the actors (usually heroes), who shape the welfare of the human community, on a raised platform; and the gods, or extra-ordinary human figures, who oversee all from their imperious remove, above the *skēnē*. All three acting areas are used in this play.

Contrary to most commentators on this play, we believe that the altar must be placed in the orchestra. If it were on the stage as is usually claimed, that narrow space would have to hold at least thirty people in the opening scene and the chorus would have to rise to the stage before the beginning of the prologue, leave for the orchestra for their first dance (the parodos, 40–88), then return to the stage after the song to supplicate Theseus (272–83), before moving down into the orchestra a final time for the first stasimon once they have released Theseus' mother (361–76). The latest full study of the play describes its "exceptionally fluid movement," (C. Collard, *Euripides, Supplices,* vol. 1 [Groningen, Neth., 1975], p. 17), but it isn't that. Such movement is dramatically incoherent and unnecessary. The only study to offer an alternative staging does away with the stage altogether (see R. Rehm, "The Staging of Suppliant Plays," *Greek, Roman, and Byzantine Studies* 29 [1988], 283–90). On the other hand, if the altar is in the orchestra, as a number of recent studies have shown is certainly possible for the fifth-century B.C. theater, (see J. P. Poe, "The Altar in the 5th Century Theater," *Classical Antiquity* 8 [1989], 116–39), interaction between chorus and actors is smooth and theatrically powerful.

When does the play begin? The opening of *Suppliant Women* reveals the nature of this problem in a most dramatic way as more than thirty people, some going to the stage, others remaining in the orchestra, arrive before the first words are spoken. Without a curtain it is hard to know when the Athenians thought that the drama "began." Does the audience consider all preliminary motion to be invisible or, as we prefer, is the pantomime before the prologue like an overture before the first words?

PROLOGUE (1–39)

A narrative prologue is a Euripidean trademark which he uses in almost a naive or primitive manner to introduce the story. Hardly a sign of poor craftsmanship, however, it serves, along with the *deus ex machina,* which closes so many Euripidean dramas, as a framing device to contain the complex twists and reversals of the Euripidean plot.

Masks and Clothing: Both Aithra and the chorus have masks and clothing which reveal that they are old women (*geraiai,* 54–56 and 34, respectively, in the Greek text), with gray hair and of noble birth. But in other respects, their costumes show marked contrast: Aithra's bright ceremonial dress clashes with the choral mourning clothes ("not meant for festivals," 97 in the Greek) and masks of shorn hair. Adrastos' *mask* (sallow to indicate misfortune and perhaps with matted hair to suggest extreme grief), as his clothing, reveals "a gray-haired man, once a glorious king" (167). He must be younger in appearance than the mothers but is bound to them in the mask's expression of grief and advanced years. The sons of the Seven wear masks of prepubescent boys which signify both royal birth and mourning. The simple outlines of a tragic mask depicting a character's age, gender, social station, and pervasive mood invite us to interpret a stage figure in generic terms, defined less as an individual person subject to psychological study than as a type perceived in broad social and religious terms.

1   The opening line introduces important words in the play: hearth-holder (in contrast with the more common epithet of city-holder for Athena) establishes Demeter's connection with house, family, and renewal. The word *chthōn* (earth) is given particular weight by its placement at the end of the line here and in five other instances in Aithra's prologue (4, 9, 17, 28, 38 in the

Greek). In its repetition, a single concept (land) used to represent different orientations opens up a whole range of concerns that the play will explore.

20–24 Adrastos lies prostrate *on the stage* in front of the doors (literally "at the gate" [104]) to Demeter's temple. The emphatic "this one here" (*hode* at 21 and 104 in the Greek) may be read as a stage direction, signifying a shift of attention from chorus to Adrastos and from orchestra to stage.

26 Both James Diggle (*Euripidis, Fabulae II,* Oxford, 1981) and Christopher Collard (*Euripides, Supplices,* Leipzig, 1984) now accept *koinon* (in common), instead of the manuscript *monon* (this task above all).

27–31 The choral lament and interruption of a fertility festival in progress threatens to pollute the entire ritual, bringing divine retribution on Attica. Far from feeling threatened by her captivity, however, Aithra responds to the women with sympathy (9–11), pity (33–34), tears and wailing of her own (284–89) and, most important, religious awe (37–8).

Aithra's sacrificing of first fruits at Eleusis is an unmistakeable allusion to the Proerosia, literally "the preliminary to the ploughing." The annual ritual at Eleusis was held on the fifth or sixth day of Pyanopsion (the latter part of October). Athens' motive for reviving and enlarging the festival circa 420 B.C. appears to be anything but reverent: citing Delphi and ancient custom, it required the cities of her empire, and invited all other Greek cities, to contribute a six-hundreth of their barley crop and a twelve-hundreth of their wheat as a first-fruit offering to the earth goddess.

PARODOS (40–88)

This is a *parodos* in name only as the chorus has already entered the theater. (For a parallel, see Aeschylus' *Eumenides.*) Aithra is in the orchestra; Adrastos and the sons of the Seven are on stage during this ode. When not entering or exiting the theater, the chorus of Greek tragedies dance in rectangular movements.

73–88 Reference to attendants here signifies most probably a semichorus, not an extra chorus (cf. 1074). Some have argued from this passage that the Chorus (fifteen in number in Euripides' day) consist of seven mothers, seven attendants, and the coryphaeus (or leader). Such precise division of roles is hardly necessary. Although the number of mothers is often listed as seven (cf. 12, 919), surely Jocasta is already dead and Amphiaraos' mother is absent. One might consider it odd if Eteoklos' mother (wife of Iphis and mother of Evadne) kept silent while her husband came on stage and her daughter committed suicide. Though all are called Argive women, Polynices' mother (Jocasta) is Theban, Tydeus' mother is Calydonian, and Parthenopaios' mother, Atalanta, is Arcadian. Nor, the audience would know, could Amphiaraos and Polynices be counted among the seven as they were already "buried" (also evident, e.g., in Adrastos' funeral praise of the five recovered corpses [819–62]). As one commentator noted, adherence to "realistic" presentation for the chorus "would be an unnecessary touch of pedantry" (N. C. Hourmouziades, *Production and Imagination in Euripides* [Athens, 1965], 81). The handmaidens must be seen as mute stage extras.

FIRST EPISODE (89–360)

89   Theseus, Aithra's son, enters near the end of the song. How are we to visualize Theseus? He is a young man, much the junior of Adrastos, but is he beardless? Aithra speaks of him frequently as "son" or "child" (*teknon*) (cf. 101, 110, 291, 300, 316, 323) and once as "my son" (*pais*, 298). Theseus, in turn, calls Aithra "Mother," both in address (284 and 330) and when referring to her (92, 93 and 355), but he also calls her "an old woman" (94). Terms of intimacy like "mother" and "son" must be considered timeless. But the chorus also call Theseus *teknon* (280), which, when used by them, must be translated "child." Earlier, however, they spoke of supplicating Theseus by touching his "cheek" (a convention often for beard) (276) and say that he is the same age as their fallen sons (282) who, we remember, also have sons who are old enough to speak and to desire revenge. Later, Theseus says that he is old enough to have survived many toils (335–36, 555; Aithra clarifies: a boar hunt, 313ff.), but the Herald counters that Theseus is "still a whelp" (*veanias*, 562). In his young manhood, he stands between the aged Adrastos and the boys of the fallen heroes. The action of this play will be his coming of age.

How regal was his appearance? Although Theseus was a legendary king of Athens and Adrastos calls him "most stout-hearted leader in all Greece,/ Lord of Athens" (164–65; see 115), Theseus himself speaks of Athens as if, contemporary with the democracy of Euripides' day, it were a free polis where "the people rule" (399–401). It would thus seem inappropriate for him to wear a crown.

89–100 Theseus enters through the *eisodos* to the spectator's right (i.e., the road from Athens). Theseus' opening words follow a typical Euripidean pattern: they begin with comments made in isolation, addressed to no one in particular (89–93), followed by visual contact, in this instance of his mother at the altar surrounded by mourners (signified at first by an *extra metrum* cry, *"ea,"* then 93–98). Only then comes the question which initiates dialogue (98–100).

103–4   It is repeatedly emphasized that the chorus encircle the altar (see 31, 94, 355–56). The area surrounding the altar must also be large enough to accommodate Aithra and temple attendants.

105   Theseus for the first time notices, or rather hears, Adrastos who is lying face down on the stage. When Aithra says, "Let them speak for themselves, my child" (110), the play takes a sudden turn as female entreaty gives way to male debate. We cannot, of course, know how the staging was managed but, with this shift in focus, it seems reasonable to imagine a corresponding shift in the place of action from orchestra to stage (at 111–12) where the new themes of rational and political deliberation will be introduced.

111–262   This is the first of the play's two debates or *agōnes*, popular in Euripidean tragedy. A fast-paced stichomythia (dialogue of alternating lines of verse, 116–63) is followed by formal argument (164–249). Theseus' severe interrogation indicates that he, unlike his mother, will *not* be swayed by pity or compassion. A *scholion* to Sophocles' *Oedipus at Colonus* (at 220) comments (it will amuse some to know) that Euripides introduced this scene "to lenghthen the drama."

132–55   In this version of the myth, Polynices leaves Thebes voluntarily to avoid fulfilling his father's curse. Tydeus was exiled from Calydon for killing his brother Melanippus in a hunting expedition. Though Tydeus claimed the death was an accident, the Calydonians suspected foul play owing to an oracle which had prophesized that Melanippus would kill him. The emblem of Thebes is a lion and that of Calydon a boar. When the two fugitives Polynices and Tydeus were dining in Argos at Adrastos' palace, they began a dispute about the glories of their respective cities. Remembering the prophecy, Adrastos married Aigeia to Polynices and Deipyla to Tydeus and promised to aid each in regaining their lost cities. At Thebes, Tydeus dies from a wound inflicted by a Theban who happened to be named Melanippus.

196–219   Theseus' theodicy. Hardly irrelevant as some have argued, critics have shown how Theseus' speech carefully rebukes Adrastos' plea point by point. Like other fifth-century B.C. theories of evolution, Theseus' view that civilization arises from a primitive, bestial state redresses the older, pessimistic view found in Hesiod's *Works and Days* (109 ff.) that civilization is characterized by a fall from piety. But this argument, which attributes the birth of civilization to the teachings of "some god," also differs from the fifth-century theories represented in Sophocles' "Ode to Man" (*Antigone* 332–71) where man is said to have taught *himself* the arts of language, agriculture, and commerce, or in Aeschylus' *Prometheus Bound* where the rebellious Prometheus, in defiance of the Olympian gods, *taught* man the above-mentioned arts and that of seeing as well.

263–71   Choral use of dialogue trimeters for more than one or two lines "marks its formal engagement in the main action" (Collard, *Euripides, Supplices,* vol. 2 [Groningen, Neth., 1975], 178).

272–83   The chorus move from orchestra to stage. These astrophic dactyls do not constitute a regular *stasimon* (i.e., they do not signify a dance), but mark extreme tension, exemplified by the fracturing of the chorus into two half-choruses (see 578–607). Similar use of lyrics outside the formal *stasima* are found in two other Euripidean "suppliant plays" but are rare in Aeschylus and Sophocles. Fluctuation in choral voice between first person singular and plural is common throughout the play and suggests that the mothers experience the agonies of despair and lament both individually and collectively. The wailing o's, e's, and a's in these lines are particularly expressive and almost impossible to capture in English.

FIRST EPISODE (SECOND PART) (284–360)

295–327   A crucial speech as Aithra mediates between the antitheses of compassion and reasoned discourse and of female and male. For the relationship between Theseus and Heracles, see commentary on ll. 1149–53, p. 76.

Theseus' filial devotion is as strong at the end of the first episode as it was at the beginning. The play will continue to explore parent/child bonds in the Iphis/Evadne episode and in the second *kommos* when the sons of the Seven swear devotion to their deceased fathers. Others have commented well on this aspect of the play; see, for example, Peter Burian, ed., in *Directions in Euripidean Criticism* (Durham, N.C., 1985): "as so often in this play, personal emotion spills over into political signification" (p. 138).

Theseus enters the orchestra and bids the chorus release his mother from the grip of their boughs. Mother, son, and Adrastos exit right, through the *eisodos*. It is at this time that the sons of the Seven probably move down into the orchestra, though others imagine this to happen at 114.

313   What we translate as "in sport," Aithra calls "a trivial labor" (*phaulon ponon*). Contrary to what she says of the boar hunt here, it was conventionally regarded as one of Theseus' famous exploits and was, for example, depicted on the metopes of the Theseion (later called the Hephaesteion) in the Athenian agora.

348–49   Theseus' claim to have established Athenian democracy is an obvious anachronism. Words with *iso-* (equal), in them, as here with "equal votes," are important throughout the play (e.g., 424–33 and 672, where "the equally-poised *agōn*" before Thebes recalls Theseus' earlier *agōn* with the Theban herald).

FIRST STASIMON (361–76)

The stage is empty for this brief ode; the sons of the Seven remain in the orchestra. The song gives Theseus time to go to Athens to win the peoples' (*dēmos*) approval and to return with an army.

SECOND EPISODE (377–577)

At the end of the first *stasimon,* Theseus and Adrastos return from Athens (right *eisodos*). In midconversation with an Athenian herald (nonspeaking part), Theseus *et al.* slowly mount the stairs to the stage where the play's second agon is about to begin.

394–565   Second agon, framed by the thwarted Athenian embassy (377–93) and Theseus' departure for war (565–77), comprises most of this episode. Formal argument (398–545) gives way to stichomythia (548–62). The mask of the Theban Herald reveals that he is older than Theseus but of lower station. The actor who previously played Aithra now plays the herald. Against earlier, and what appear to be conventional, treatments of this story (i.e., Aeschylus' *Eleusinians*; cf. Plutarch's *Theseus* 29.4ff.), Euripides chooses to resolve tensions between Athens and Thebes by war. Contrary to most of the "suppliant" plays, the herald here does not attempt to seige the suppliants by force.

It is a mistake to read Theseus as an idealized but poorly disguised portrait of Pericles, Athens' great ruler, recently dead from the plague, who (paraphrasing Thucydides 2.65.9) governed a city democratic in name but monarchical in nature. To see this young Theseus as a mature politician ignores the important lessons he learns about religion, ancient law, and persuasion and fails to acknowledge his initiation into manhood through the experience of war.

430–33   John Milton, who read and annotated Euripides extensively, was particularly struck by these lines, placing them on the title page of his *Areopagitica* (1644).

469–82   No Greek author spoke more passionately than Euripides about the horrors of war, the cause of peace, and the abuse of those defeated in war (see *Hecuba, The Trojan Women*), and no one better championed the cause of women and the politically oppressed (see *Medea*). However, Euripides cannot easily be considered a pacifist (see *Heracleidae*) or a staunch defender of women's rights (again the *Medea*; the once-sympathetic chorus's uncomprehending horror at Medea by play's end; cf. the female chorus's joy in Dionysus' brutal revenge in *The Bacchae*).

484–85 Euripides puns on Capaneus' name, as if from "Smoke Man," implying his death from Zeus' thunderbolt was fated.

559 These lines acknowledge Athens' most famous characteristic: its meddling in other's affairs, a quality variously admired or regarded as arrogance leading to the city's ruin.

SECOND STASIMON (IAMBIC TRIMETERS PREDOMINANTLY) (578–607)

Adrastos remains on stage; the sons of the Seven in the orchestra. Like the last song, this one "marks time" while Theseus is away at war. It is rare in Greek tragedy for a chorus in a formal *stasimon* to break up, as here, into hemichoruses (see 272–83). Euripides deviates from conventional form to reveal the mothers' great anxiety over the outcome of war.

THIRD EPISODE (608–740)

At the end of the last song, a messenger arrives from Thebes and rushes to the stage to announce the news of Athenian victory. Captured earlier in Adrastos' attack against Thebes, but now freed by Theseus, the Argive messenger is able both to criticize Adrastos' conduct in the first war and to praise Theseus' in the second. The mask for this Argive citizen of indeterminate age will reveal, most probably, a male of the middle class (see 243–45). He is played by the actor who played the Theban Herald and Aithra. Euripides was a master of the messenger's report (a tragic convention of reporting offstage events, like battles and violent deaths, which were unsuitable for the theater), and brought the form to new heights. A technique which he used in all but one of his extant plays, the messenger's speech in this play is particularly fine for its relatively unordained style, rapid pace, and epic flavor. The word that we translate as "watch" (625) in Greek is *theatēs* (observer or spectator), as if the messenger were recounting a theatrical performance.

623–38 The Athenian army, divided according to infantry (627), cavalry (633), and chariots (634) into three detachments (626), surrounds Thebes, as the Argive army did in its attack according to Aeschylus' *Seven against Thebes*. The infantry invests the area south of the walls from the Ismenean hill in the southeast (628) to the fountain of Ares in the southwest (632); the chariots occupy the area to the north of the walls where Amphion's tomb is found (635). The cavalry, in detachments of equal size (634), take positions to the east and west of the walls. The messenger, located at the Electran gate in the eastern portion of the city, claims that he was able to *see* the chariots which only seems possible if they moved southward in the course of the battle (653–54). Theseus commanded the right wing of the Athenian infantry in the southeast, not far from the Electran gate. For the battle reconstruction, see James Diggle, "The *Supplices* of Euripides," *Greek, Roman, and Byzantine Studies* 14 (1973), 252–63.

677   Claiming descent from the dragon's teeth sown by Cadmus, the Cadmeans (or Thebans) were known as Spartoi (Sown Men).

679–82   For the Epidaurian club, see 1149–53.

692 ff.   The praise of Theseus here corrects what the Theban Herald had said about brash young leaders and instead identifies Theseus with the wise and brave (cf. 496–98).

699   Although on stage since 377, Adrastos has not spoken since 262, except for the beginning of a speech interrupted by Theseus (501). He is likely that he leaves the stage, along with the Messenger, at the end of the episode (740). His purpose will be to herald in the corpses.

703 ff.   Eteokles' offer of compromise is not attested elsewhere. Euripides invents the story to illustrate further Argos' aggressive and unwarranted attack against Thebes.

THIRD STASIMON (741–56)

In iambic dimeters and trimeters, this song sets the mood of lamentation that marks choral sentiments for the remainder of the play. The structure of that lament follows closely the pattern of Greek funerary mourning: the carrying out of the corpses with attendant mourners, graveside eulogy, cremation, presentation of the ashes with further choral lamentation (third *stasimon* and first *kommos*, Adrastos' funeral oration, final *kommos*). Although choral lyric comprises less than a seventh of the lines in the first half of the play, it dominates the second half, comprising close to a third of the lines. The sons of the Seven remain in the orchestra for this song.

FOURTH EPISODE (757–909)

757–96   First *kommos* (literally a striking, especially a beating of the breasts, *kommos* in tragedy refers to a song sung alternately by an actor and the chorus, usually in a mournful dirge) is set off by Adrastos' arrival, with Athenian ball-bearers, of the five recovered bodies. Initial anapests (757–60) as the corpses arrive give way to a meter similar to that in the last song, though more frequent resolutions and suppressions of iambs mark increased passion. If we are right, Adrastos moves to the stage with the bodies; the mothers and sons remain in the orchestra.

798–800 Textual corruption here requires some guesswork in the translation.

806–816 These lines have been interpreted as a Euripidean sneer at the general convention of messenger speeches. More probably, they serve the needs of the play, pointing out the purpose of Theseus' request.

FOURTH STASIMON (IN AEOLICS) (910–34)

For the first time in the play, the chorus sing in a theater empty of all other characters. The subsequent scene with its new characters and fresh plot will be free from all visual associations with the main plot.

FIFTH EPISODE (935–1064)

935–85 Anapests (935–44) for Evadne's arrival lead into her lyric monody (945–85), a favorite form in Euripidean dramaturgy to express intense emotion for an actor (in aeolics, linking this song to the ode in front of it). The strophe is separated from the antistrophe by a choral utterance in iambic trimeters (962–64). In later experiments with this form, Euripides will abandon the strophic structure altogether, presumably because the formal balance of strophe and antistrophe was felt to inhibit the unbridled emotional outburst characteristic of the monody. Aristophanes in *The Frogs* (1331 ff.) brilliantly parodies these scenes.

Evadne is played, most likely, by the same actor who plays Theseus. Her mask, like Theseus', shows a young adult of noble standing and, like her attire, conveys joy, not mourning.

939–44 Evadne enters high up on a cliff overlooking the temple precinct. In a personal discussion (December 10, 1991) William Arrowsmith suggested that Evadne's joy speaks of a person unhinged, made mad from grief. As such, she would be another of Euripides' women who are victims of unendurable pain.

How did she enter? Scholars seem agreed that it would be aesthetically unacceptable for both Evadne and Athena to appear as *deae ex machina*. But, as hinted in the introduction, the two may interestingly be compared as both are above the human world and insensitive to it, both display something of a military outlook (see Evadne's language), and both defend violent action whether in the form of suicide or an insistence on revenge. Of course, differences between the two are equally significant: one is mortal and in love with death, the other is divine; one is motivated by eros, the other by political imperative. Perhaps it is best, finally, to see them occupying distinct spaces. Either could arrive on the *machina* or appear on the *theologeion,* and both possibilities have been proposed for each figure, but it is certainly easier to imagine Evadne leaping into the pyre from the stage building than from the *machina.* As Peter Burian has pointed out in personal correspondence (October 1, 1993), late Euripides appears to be fond of human characters appearing from the *theologeion,* as exampled by Antigone in the *Phoenician Women* and the mad tableau at the end of the *Orestes.*

986 Iphis is played, most probably, by the same actor who plays Adrastos. His mask, like Adrastos' and those of the chorus, shows an aged man of noble standing in extreme grief. The visual contrast between the masks of Evadne and Iphis must have been haunting. Feeling a grief analogous to that of the mothers, Iphis most probably remains in the orchestra for the entire scene, where he will also have a better view of Evadne. Iphis' wife, we recall, is also one of the seven mothers of the chorus.

1011 The phrase "glory in victory" (*kallinikos*) recalls Adrastos' "glorious in victory" (*kallinike*) to praise Theseus at 114.

1021–23 A fair number of young women in Euripides commit suicide, not so much as Phaedra in the *Hippolytus* to escape shame, but as a female form of heroism (cf. Iphigeneia in the *Iphigeneia at Aulis,* Macaria in *Heracleidae,* Praxithea's daughter in *Erechtheus* [a fragment], and Laodamia in *Protesilaus* [a fragment]). No suicide is more vainglorious and meaningless than Evadne's in the *Suppliant Women.* The most noble of all these self-sacrificers, who dies for honor and to escape shame, is Polyxena in *Hecuba.* In *Heracles Mad,* suicide is seen as a less heroic path than that of facing one's shame. Almost certainly, Evadne jumps to a pyre offstage.

1024–31 The short second *kommos.* As Evadne leaps, the chorus and Iphis break into agitated dochmii, formally joining them in their shared feelings of horror and loss.

1065–16 The third (or final) *kommos.* The chorus announce in anapests (1065–73) the return of the sons of the Seven with the ashes. At 1074, the sons, a secondary chorus, first on stage (1–360) and then in the orchestra (361–900) before they leave to cremate the remains of their fathers, move back to the stage and speak for the first time. Rather than regard this long silence "as one of the many weaknesses in Euripides' *Suppliants,* a play with none of the intensity or scenic and dramatic economy of Aeschylus' *Suppliants,*" as Oliver Taplin says in *The Stagecraft of Aeschylus* (Oxford, 1977), 236–37, we believe it is a masterful stroke. Economical in its clear imitation of, and divergence from, the first *kommos,* intense in its testimony that the buried dead are still very much alive and to be feared (see 526–31), scenic and visual in its portrayal of the unbridgeable gulf between orchestra and stage, expressed here as the gulf between the desire for peace and the blood urge for revenge.

A number of plays in Greek tragedy have a secondary chorus, but Euripides is the only tragedian to give speaking parts to children. As here, all instances occur in lyrics.

1074–1112   There are many textual difficulties in these lines, but the most serious problem concerns the designation of parts for primary and secondary chorus. In this, we deviate from Collard (1984) and follow Diggle (*Euripidis, Fabulae II,* 1981).

EXODUS (1117–84)

It is a signature of Euripidean dramaturgy to conclude with a divine epiphany or an epilogue (in nine of his seventeen extant plays), but no divine appearance is more abrupt than this one. Athena is played by the same actor who played Aithra (and the Theban Herald and Argive Messenger). For her entrance, see 939–44. Her mask, perhaps imitating the ivory and gold cult statue of *Athena Parthenos* in the Parthenon completed by Phidias in 438 B.C., signifies her divinity.

1149–53   Heracles' tripod. As often in Attic mythology, Theseus is a double of Heracles, here suggested by reference to Theseus' boar hunt, his Epidaurian club like Heracles' telltale weapon, and the tripod which Heracles won at Troy and gave to Theseus to dedicate at Delphi. Has Theseus been remiss in his obligations? The story appears to be another Euripidean invention. As the tripod in the past marked Theseus' debt to, and bond with, Heracles, so now it testifies to Adrastos' debt and obligation to Theseus.

1163   For the reading "by the road to Argos" we follow an emendation suggested by B. Heath in 1762, accepted by Collard (1984), but not by Diggle (1981). There are several manuscript difficulties with the line, not the least of which is the reading *theou* (of the god), in place of Heath's *hodou* (road.) But it is not at all certain what deity is meant; suggestions range from Hecate to Poseidon to Metaneira to Leucothea. Others read *theōi* (to the god), referring to Apollo. Road makes good sense: the exact location of the *temenos* marking the pyres of the dead (except for Capaneus who is buried in Demeter's sacred precinct, 942–44) and the placement of the buried sacrificial knife is unspecified, but as Collard remarks no place would be more suitable than the fork where the road from the Isthmus divides, one leading to Thebes, the other along the coast to Athens (Collard, *Euripides, Supplices,* vol. 2 [Groningen, Neth., 1975], 417–18).

1173   The image of the Epigoni as lion cubs recalls the oracle in which Apollo instructed Adrastos to wed his daughters to a boar and a lion (see 141). Calling humans *skumnoi,* used of young animals (whelp, puppy, etc.), is common in Euripides and deliberate, as it suggests a bestial ferocity and emnity, as well as courage, in man when the young mature.

1182–84   It is the convention in Greek tragedy that the chorus march out of the theater to mark the close.

GLOSSARY

ADRASTOS: king of Argos and commander-in-chief of the Seven against Thebes. He alone escaped from that expedition alive, in large measure because of his speedy horse, Areion, begotten when Demeter took the form of a mare and Poseidon that of a stallion (in the mountains of Arcadia). His son Aigialeus was the only one of the Epigoni, or sons of the Seven, to die when they attacked Thebes.

AIGEUS: former king of Athens. The son of Pandion, he married Aithra; Theseus was their offspring.

AIGIALEUS: son of Adrastos. Avenging the defeat of the Seven against Thebes, he was the first to lead the sons of the Seven in a renewed assault against Thebes. Although the assault was successful, he was killed, causing his father to die of grief.

AITHRA: daughter of Pittheus; as wife of Aigeus, she begets Theseus. It is a Euripidean invention, it appears, to include her in the Argive supplication of Theseus and the Athenians to recover the Argive war dead at Thebes.

AMPHIARAOS: an Argive hero and seer; son of Oikles, brother-in-law of Adrastos, married to Eriphyle. Polynices bribed Eriphyle to persuade her husband to take part in the expedition against Thebes although Amphiaraos foresaw that all but Adrastos would die in that battle. When the others were killed and Amphiaraos was fleeing from the field, Zeus threw a thunderbolt in front of him, opening a chasm into which Amphiaraos, his chariot and his charioteer vanished. To avenge this death, Amphiaraos' son Alkmaion sacked Thebes and slew Eriphyle. In death, Amphiaraos became a chthonian god of healing and oracles, his most extensive shrine being that of Zeus Amphiaraos near Psophis in the north central part of the Peloponnesos.

AMPHION: a Theban hero who, with Zethus, built the walls of Thebes by playing the lyre. His grave was near the North Gate. See commentary at 623–38.

APOLLO: Olympian god of prophecy, the healing arts, lyric poetry, discursive speech; son of Zeus and Leto. In *Suppliant Women* he is mentioned as the oracular voice at the sanctuary of Delphi.

ARES: Olympian god of war and the personification of strife; son of Zeus and Hera.

ARGOS: city in the northeastern part of the Peloponnesos and the state for much of the northern Peloponnesos. Adrastos is its king.

ARGIVE: those from Argos.

ARTEMIS: Olympian goddess of the hunt and the wild, of chastity and childbirth; daughter of Zeus and Leto, and Apollo's twin.

ATHENA: or Pallas Athena, Olympian goddess of wisdom, tutelary deity of Athens; parthenogenic daughter of Zeus.

ATHENS: the city of Attica, where Theseus is king.

CAPANEUS: an Argive and one of the Seven against Thebes; he married Evadne. When scaling the walls of Thebes and boasting that not even Zeus could keep him from burning the city, he was struck by Zeus with a thunderbolt and toppled from the scaling ladder. See commentary at 484–85.

CITHAERON: mountain range separating Boeotia from Attica and the plain of Eleusis.

CREON: king of Thebes; Oedipus' uncle (by marriage).

DEA EX MACHINA: (Latin: goddess from the machine): the crane in the Greek theater which lifted actors aloft.

DELPHI: a town and sanctuary in central Greece, most important of Apollo's oracular sites.

DEMETER: Olympian goddess of fertility, grain, and renewal; Zeus' sister. At Eleusis she was honored in the Lesser and Greater Mysteries (in the spring and autumn, respectively), festivals of death and renewal. Also at Eleusis, worshiped at the Proerosia with her daughter, Persephone.

ELEUSIS: a town and sanctuary in Attica, about eleven miles west of Athens; famous for its chthonic site of Demeter.

ELEUTHERAE: town on the southern slope of Mount Cithaeron where there was a pass through the mountain from the plain of Eleusis to Boeotia. The site is also the home of Dionysos Eleuthereus (the cult god of the Theater of Dionysos), whose cult statue (a pillar-shaped idol of the god) was transported from here to Athens as a prelude to the Great Dionysia.

EPIDAURIAN MACE: see commentary at 1148–53.

ETEOKLES: Theban king, son of Oedipus and Jocasta, brother of Polynices. See Polynices.

ETEOKLOS: an Argive and one of the Seven; son of Iphis, brother of Evadne.

EVADNE: daughter of Iphis and sister of Eteoklos. She married Capaneus. See commentary at 939–44.

HADES: god of the underworld; Zeus' brother; Persephone's husband. His name may also refer to the Underworld itself.

HERACLES: son of Zeus and the mortal Alkmene; most famous of the Greek heroes. Indentured to Eurystheus, king of Tiryns in the Argolid, he was compelled to undertake the famous twelve labors (frequently called *ponoi*, [pains] in Greek). See commentary at 1148–53.

HIPPOMEDON: an Argive and one of the Seven; Adrastos' brother. His son, Polydorus, was one of the sons of the Seven.

INACHOS: son of Ocean; he gave his name to the River Inachos, near Argos.

IPHIS: an Argive; father of Evadne and Eteoklos, who was one of the Seven against Thebes.

KORE: (maiden): see Persephone.

MAENAD: (mad): frenzied female worshiper of Dionysos.

PANHELLENIC: (all Greek): term used to refer to the laws, customs, and festivals common to all Greeks.

PANDION: eighth king of Athens, the second by this name; Aigeus' father.

PALLAS: see Athena.

PARTENOPAIOS: son of Meleager and Atalanta, from Arcadia (in other versions Adrastos' brother). Because of her affection for Atalanta, Artemis gave Parthenopaios heavenly arrows and showered him with ambrosia, but these gifts did little to save him from a huge stone hurled from the ramparts at Thebes.

PELOPONNESOS: (also spelled Peloponnese), Greece's southern peninsula.

PERSEPHONE: goddess of the underworld; daughter of Zeus and Demeter. Zeus gave her in marriage to Hades, an act Demeter regarded as a rape and a death.

PITTHEUS: king of the Troizen; Aithra's father. Renowned for his wisdom and eloquence; also respected as a seer. He arranged for Aigeus, returning from Delphi, to sleep with Aithra by getting him drunk.

POLYNICES: a Theban and one of the Seven; son of Oedipus and Jocasta, brother of Eteokles, Antigone, and Ismene. As he was dying from Eteokles' hand, he mortally wounded his brother in the heart.

PROEROSIA: (a preliminary to the plowing): annual festival to Demeter and Persephone held at Eleusis on the fifth or sixth day of Pyanopsion (late October). See commentary at 27–31.

SEVEN AGAINST THEBES: led by Adrastos to help Polynices regain the throne from Eteokles. When all but Adrastos had been killed, Thebes refused to release the corpses for burial. The Seven include: Polynices, Tydeus, Amphiaraos, Capaneus, Eteoklos, Hippomedon, and Parthenopaios. See commentary at 73–88.

SONS OF THE SEVEN: known as the Epigoni (the after-born), who, in vengeance of their fathers' deaths, captured and plundered the city of Thebes. The oracle at Delphi promised them success if Alkmaion, son of Amphiaraos, should lead them, which he did do, although reluctantly, after Aigialeus' death.

THEBES: the largest city in Boeotia, renowned as the home of Cadmos and for its seven city gates; Creon is its king.

THEOLOGEION: (place for divine address): atop the stage building. See commentary at orchestra and stage (pp. 65–66).

THESEUS: greatest hero of the Athenians and one of their early kings; son of Aigeus (or Poseidon) and Aithra. See commentary at 89, 394–565.

TYDEUS: son of Oineus, king of Calydon; one of the Seven Argive captains. As he was dying, Athena intended to make him immortal but had a change of heart when she saw him eating out the brain of the man who had struck him a mortal wound. See commentary at 73–88, 132–55.

ZEUS: king of the Olympian gods; married to Hera.